W9-BZX-519

BEYOND THE PASSION

BEYOND THE PASSION

Rethinking the Death and Life of Jesus

Stephen J. Patterson

Fortress Press
Minneapolis

BEYOND THE PASSION

Copyright © 2004 Augsburg Fortress. All rights reserved. Except for brief quotations in critical articles or reviews, no part of this book may be reproduced in any manner without prior written permission from the publisher. Write: Permissions, Augsburg Fortress, Box 1209, Minneapolis, MN 55440-1209.

Unless otherwise noted, Scripture quotations are from the New Revised Standard Version Bible, copyright © 1989 by the Division of Christian Education of the National Council of the Churches of Christ in the USA, and are used by permission.

Cover and book design: Zan Ceeley

Library of Congress Cataloging-in-Publication Data
Patterson, Stephen J.
  Beyond the Passion : rethinking the death and life of Jesus / Stephen J. Patterson.
    p. cm.
  ISBN 0-8006-3674-0 (pbk. : alk. paper)—ISBN 0-8006-6091-9 (hardcover with jacket : alk. paper)
  1. Jesus Christ—Biography. I. Title.
  BT301.3.P38 2004
  232.9′01—dc22
                                                        2004011584

The paper used in this publication meets the minimum requirements of American National Standard for Information Sciences—Permanence of Paper for Printed Library Materials, ANSI Z329.48-1984.

Manufactured in the U.S.A.
08   07   06   05   04   1   2   3   4   5   6   7   8   9   10

For
John Warren Patterson
1931–2004

Contents

Epilogue: The Resurrection of a Nobody   103

Killing Jesus (A Conclusion)   123

Abbreviations

AB	Anchor Bible
ABD	*Anchor Bible Dictionary.* Ed. D. N. Freedman. 6 vols. New York: Doubleday, 1992
alt.	altered translation
ANF	*Ante-Nicene Fathers*
Ant.	Josephus, *Antiquities of the Jews*
BHT	Beiträge zur historischen Theologie
CBQ	*Catholic Biblical Quarterly*
CIL	*Corpus Inscriptiones Latinarum.* Berlin: Reimer, 1893–
FCBS	Fortress Classics in Biblical Studies
FRLANT	Forschungen zur Religion und Literatur des Alten und Neuen Testaments
HDR	Harvard Dissertations in Religion
HNT	Handbuch zum Neuen Testament
HR	*History of Religions*
HTR	*Harvard Theological Review*
HTS	Harvard Theological Studies
JSNTSup	Journal for the Study of the New Testament Supplement Series
LCL	Loeb Classical Library
LSJ	H. G. Liddell, Robert Scott, H. Stuart Jones, and Roderick McKenzie, *Greek-English Lexicon,* 9th edition, with supplement. Oxford: Clarendon, 1968
MT	Masoretic text
NRSV	New Revised Standard Version
NTAbh	Neutestamentliche Abhandlungen
NTS	*New Testament Studies*
NTTS	New Testament Tools and Studies
OGIS	*Orientis Graeci Inscriptiones Selectae.* Ed. W. Dittenberger. 2 vols. Reprint. Hildesheim: Olms, 1960
OTP	*The Old Testament Pseudepigrapha.* Ed. James H. Charlesworth. 2 vols. Garden City, N.Y.: Doubleday, 1983–1985
PNTC	Pelican New Testament Commentaries
RB	*Revue biblique*
SBLDS	Society of Biblical Literature Dissertation Series

SBS	Stuttgarter Bibelstudien
SHR	Studies in the History of Religions
SIG	*Sylloge inscriptionum graecarum.* Ed. W. Dittenberger. 3d ed. 4 vols. Leipzig: Olms, 1915–24
SJ	Studia Judaica
SJLA	Studies in Judaism in Late Antiquity
SNTSMS	Society for New Testament Studies Monograph Series
ThQ	*Theologische Quartalschrift*
TRE	*Theologische Realenzyklopädie.* Ed. G. Krause and G. Müller. Berlin: de Gruyter, 1977–
War	Josephus, *The Jewish War*
ZNW	*Zeitschrift für die neutestamentliche Wissenschaft und die Kunde der älteren Kirche*

Introduction

Is Jesus Dead?

Is Jesus dead? It ought to have been a simple question. Jesus lived—and died—almost two thousand years ago. He was executed by the Roman governor of Palestine in about the year 35 C.E. Of course he is dead. He is not alive somewhere today, living incognito in the south of France. We will not be spotting Jesus ordering a hamburger in a McDonald's restaurant in Nairobi. He is a figure of the past. He is dead.

Yet if someone were to ask this simple question today, many would find it difficult to answer with a simple yes or no. One might not even have to be a Christian for the question to sound slightly odd. Christian or not, just about everyone associates the name of Jesus with claims of resurrection. For believers, merely to entertain the thought "Is Jesus dead?" will be more than a little discomfiting—a flirtation, even, with blasphemy. Could he be dead? Certainly not! "Jesus is alive!" we Christians say. "God raised him from the dead!" Then he is alive? With a little thought, questions arise. If we say Jesus is alive, in what sense precisely do we imagine this to be true? *Might* we expect to spot him ordering a hamburger in a McDonald's? A silly thought; Jesus is not Elvis. Many believers might say that Jesus is alive, but in

1

heaven with God. If one believes in heaven as a place where people go when they die, this may seem sensible. If heaven awaits the dead, then we might well say that Jesus ended up there too. But we would not consider all of those dearly departed saints of heaven to be *alive*. They are dead, or, more delicately, "They have passed away." Has Jesus passed away? This too sounds odd, I suspect.

The question, "Is Jesus dead?" certainly sounded odd to me. It came at the end of a talk I was giving on the life of Jesus, posed by someone who, as it turned out, was troubled by the fact that my discussion had not included a single word about the resurrection. What Jesus said, the things that he did—these historical matters were quite interesting, but ultimately not very important. The life of Jesus, after all, ended in death. For most Christian believers, what is truly remarkable and important about Jesus is not his life, but his resurrection from the dead. Jesus' death is significant not as the end of Jesus' life, but as the first half of the saving event that comprises the Christian gospel: the death and resurrection of Jesus. This great divine cosmic event, around which all of human history pivots, is what saves us from our sins. Apart from this, the death of Jesus would simply be the meaningless end to an interesting but insignificant life. I soon came to understand that "Is Jesus dead?" really meant "So what?"

In this book I intend to challenge this "So what?" One of the great mistakes of Christian theology has been our attempt to understand the death and resurrection of Jesus apart from his life. The first followers of Jesus generally did not do this. All four of the New Testament Gospels tell of Jesus' death as part of the story of his life. His death and resurrection are directly related to his life; they issue from it. In the Gospels, Jesus is put to death for the things he says and does. God then raises him from the dead to undo the injustice done to Jesus, and to place a divine stamp of approval on the words and deeds of Jesus as the words and deeds of a genuine Son of God. This pattern of thinking belongs to the ancient tradition of martyrdom. In this tradition, death and resurrection do not stand alone. Indeed, apart from the life of the martyr, in which comes to expression all that he or she stands for, the cause for which the martyr was willing to die, the death of the martyr has no meaning. Left to itself, the martyr's violent death becomes nothing more than a focus for sadomasochistic passions, or perhaps a tableau to satisfy our prurient fascinations with human violence and death.

Imagine, if you will, celebrating the annual Martin Luther King Jr. holiday simply by fixing our gaze once again on King's death. Over and over again we would replay the film footage of his assassination at the Lorraine Hotel in Memphis. Scholars and preachers might focus on his final twelve hours, his last meal, what he wore, his dying words. They might reflect on the significance of the weapon that killed him, his time of death, or the sort of casket in which he was laid out. Perhaps the actual moment of his death could be re-created and filmed. Imagine spending the holiday like this, all the while saying nothing about King's life. No interest in his great manifesto, "I Have a Dream." No concern for such great prophecies as the "Letter from a Birmingham Jail." Not a word about civil rights, desegregation, the Vietnam War, or King's vision of peace and justice in a world torn by violence and hatred. To celebrate his death apart from the cause for which he lived would be ridiculous and meaningless.

Yet this is what we have done for the most part with Jesus. For most Christians the Apostles' Creed is quite sufficient: Jesus was born of the Virgin Mary, suffered under Pontius Pilate, was crucified, dead, and buried. After the Virgin Birth we leap over Jesus' life to take in his death in all its significance, as if it could be significant without a life to make it so. But so it has become to us: his death is the sacrifice that ensures our forgiveness before a God torn between anger and compassion. What need do we have of his life if it is his death that ensures our salvation? But this was not so for the earliest friends and followers of Jesus. They were profoundly devoted to his way of life, and they used his death to call attention to his life. They did not see his death or his resurrection as events significant in themselves. They were the fitting end of a life of extraordinary power and vision, a life to be embraced and remembered as epiphanic. Virtually every word spoken about the death of Jesus among his first followers was calculated to resurrect the significance of Jesus' life for those who loved him, and would come to love him in the years ahead. They spoke of the movement he began as "the way"—his way of life.

I have arranged the material that follows into three basic sections, each with a focus on a distinct early Christian understanding of Jesus' death: Jesus as "Victim," as "Martyr," and as "Sacrifice." I will treat these categories separately, but they are interrelated. Each overlaps with and is woven into the others to create a loose, if complex, web of meaning surrounding Jesus' death. These strands are nonetheless worth pulling apart so that one may see them for themselves and so understand their distinctive contributions more clearly. In many ways these strands represent familiar territory for us, and into them are woven some of our most cherished ideas about Jesus' death, such as the atonement. But as I revisited these ancient Christian ideas for myself, and examined them in their ancient context, I encountered many surprising things long forgotten and lost under the great pile of medieval atonement theology with which most Christians are burdened today. In the end, I hope to show that these three strands, though distinct, work together to point the would-be follower of Jesus back to his life—to his words, his deeds, and his fate—as a life to be embraced as *the* life, and a fate to call one's own.

Is Jesus dead? It is not a simple question. The earliest friends and followers of Jesus did not answer it with a simple yes or no. They pondered the question, as they pondered the fate of the one they had come to love. They thought about who killed him and why. They thought about the God they had come to know through him, and through the Jewish traditions of their ancestors, and they considered how such a God would react to this tragic, brutal event. They also thought about the fact that even though Jesus was dead, he was not dead *to them*. His spirit was still coursing through their veins. How was this so? What did it mean?

Prologue

The Crucifixion of a Nobody

Hope is not always history, and neither is hyperbole.
In this case, as so often before and after, horror is history.
—John Dominic Crossan, *Who Killed Jesus?*

What Happened to Jesus?

Before we can begin to understand and appreciate the early Christian response to the death of Jesus, we must first have some realistic idea of what happened to him. This is difficult for Christians. From the time we are old enough to understand the stories of the Christian faith, read to us from the pulpit Bible in the tiniest of churches to the great cathedrals, we have seen the events of Jesus' final days unfold before us like a great pageant. Jesus comes to Jerusalem to challenge his enemies, the chief priests, the scribes, and the Pharisees. They have plotted all along to gain his demise. Now he plays right into their hands. He does so deliberately. He knows his fate ahead of time—how he is to be betrayed by one of his own, arrested, tortured, crucified, and after three days rise from the dead. It is all part of God's plan to save us from our sins, which the old religion of the Jews, the religion of law and legalism, could not do.

Thus rendered in this mixture of text and tradition, the death of Jesus is not a calamity, or even a surprise. It is the result of a well-executed, successful plan to create what we know today as the Christian religion. It is a great triumph, not a tragedy. In the end, it is not just Christ's triumph we celebrate in this story, but our own as well. The story of Jesus' death and resurrection has been central to Christians' understanding of themselves over against Jews. His death symbolizes their rejection of the Messiah; his resurrection signals that we are right, they were/are wrong.[1]

But this was not how Jesus' first followers actually experienced his death. This story comes from writers and theologians a generation removed from the actual events surrounding Jesus' death. It was created during a time of great animosity between Jews and those who followed Jesus (by then a group comprising both Jews and Gentiles). It presupposes a great deal of theological reflection on the ultimate significance of Jesus and his fate. Told in context, it can become a powerful and moving story. But it is seldom told in this way—as a story in context. It is usually presented as history, that is, *what really happened*. In fact, I have never heard the story of Good Friday presented to a congregation in a way that did not at least imply its utter historicity. The worst consequence of this has been the legacy of Christian anti-Semitism that has grown from the mistaken notion that "the Jews" were responsible for the death of Jesus. This is one of the great lies of Western civilization, and the origin of unfathomable evil. But a second consequence has had to do more with Christians themselves and their understanding of Jesus and his meaning for our lives. As a story whose content is supplied by theological reflection, it does not turn out to be a very realistic story from a human point of view. It is the story of the death of a god, not of a human being. As such, it can be difficult to connect with as a real human experience.

I can recall seeing cracks in the historical facade placed on this story already as a child hearing it again and again. Why, for example, if Jesus' death was part of God's greater plan, is Judas not worshiped as a saint rather than vilified as a traitor? Or why, if Jesus knew what was happening all the time, did he cry out from the cross with his last breath, "My God, my God, why have you forsaken me?" (Mark 15:34). Or how shall we view the dramatic scene in Gethsemane, in which Jesus prays that he might be delivered from what must soon take place (Mark 14:32-42)? Is this reported history? How would the author have known what Jesus said on that occasion? From the story we learn that the only witnesses, the disciples, were asleep. And what of the trial scenes? In Mark, the only witnesses present—the Jewish leadership of Jerusalem—are hostile (14:55-65; 15:1-5). How did Mark come by so many details that would impugn their role in the matter? Or who could have reported on the private conversation between Pilate and Jesus in the Johannine account of the trial (John 18:33-38)? And what reconnaissance produced the communiqué between Pilate and his wife concerning her dreams (Matt 27:19)?

In due course we shall return to the biblical stories and other traditions attached to Jesus' death, to read them in context as early Christian attempts to give meaning to the dramatic end of his life. They are not history but interpretations of a history, told from the vantage point of an omniscient narrator. But in order to appreciate all that these stories are trying to accomplish, we must begin somewhere else—with the event they are trying to interpret: the death of Jesus. What do we really know about what happened to him? We have but a few facts with which to work, but they can tell us quite a lot.

Crucifixion

We know that Jesus was crucified, probably around Passover, in Jerusalem, by order of the Roman prefect of Judea, Pontius Pilate. This is not much information, but it tells us something significant about Jesus and why he was killed.

Crucifixion was in Jesus' day Rome's trademark means of executing peasants involved in seditious activity against the empire.[2] The Romans did not invent it—the Persians and Carthaginians used it before them to punish errant generals and governors. But one might say the Romans perfected it as the ultimate weapon of terror and intimidation. They did not use it against errant leaders, but against slaves and peasants. They used it against common criminals to deter crime. They used it in laying siege to cities, crucifying enemy captives in plain sight of those inside the city walls in an attempt to demoralize and break the will of the enemy by this gruesome display. But most importantly, they used it to punish peasant rebels in outlying districts. Sometimes leaders were crucified individually; sometimes whole groups were crucified en masse. For example, when Jesus would still have been a small child, a peasant insurrection broke out across Palestine when Herod died and the Jews feared that his much-loathed sons would be given to rule over Palestine. Varus, the Roman general in charge of quashing the rebellion, burned to the ground the towns of Sepphoris, Sappho, and Emmaus, and sold their inhabitants into slavery. Afterward his army searched the countryside for those who had escaped and had them crucified—about two thousand in all— their writhing, tortured bodies providing the necessary message.[3] At the start of the Jewish War (66 C.E.) the Roman governor of Judea, Florus, crucified 3,600 people, including children and infants.[4] Jesus was not the only person to die on a Roman cross. Thousands of peasants suffered this same fate in his day. Crucifixion was highly organized, massive state terrorism,[5] intended to intimidate the vast peasant and slave populations of the empire into passivity. Its record of success is rather impressive. The Roman *Pax* was seldom interrupted by insurrection during the period of the empire, and when unrest did break out, it was usually short-lived.

What does this tell us about the death of Jesus? It tells us that his executioners were Roman, not Jewish. To be sure, Rome could not control a province like Judea without high-level local collaboration. In Jesus' day the high priesthood would have been co-opted entirely by Rome. But this does not get Pilate off the hook. The cross of Jesus was a Roman cross. History cannot get any plainer than this. One of the great ironies of history, it turns out, is that for centuries Gentile Christians have blamed Jews for the death of Jesus, when in fact it was a Gentile official of a Gentile state who had Jesus, a Jew, executed like so many other Jews of his day.

It also tells us that his crime was sedition against the Roman state. This implication is often dismissed on the grounds that Jesus' message was a "religious" one, not "political." But in the ancient world there was no such distinction between religion and politics. The empire was divinely ordained, the emperor God's Son. Worship was to the gods Roma and Augustus. In Judea, Roman tribute may even have been collected in collaboration with the high priest.[6] Jesus could not speak of a new kingdom, an empire of God, without implicating the religious *and* political structures that dominated his life. The preaching of Jesus undermined these structures completely. The suspicion that his ideas were seditious to the Roman Empire was not mistaken.

It tells us also that he was regarded by his executioners as nothing, a peasant nobody who had the unmitigated temerity to challenge the great Roman *Pax*. But this nobody could be used. The manner of his death could intimidate others who might be inspired by what he did. He was crucified as a warning to others: this is what happens to people who might be tempted to think as he dared to think.

What was so intimidating about crucifixion? Quite simply, it was a very slow, agonizing, public way to die. If the victim was flogged, or otherwise tortured prior to the actual crucifixion, death might come more quickly. But victims of the cross might also survive for days, as exposure to the elements, animals, and unkind passersby gradually wore them down. The fear, delirium, loss of control over bodily function all would have contributed to the shame of the peasant victim. Death might come by shock, exposure, or sometimes suffocation, as the weight of the victim's body forced it to collapse in upon itself, making it more and more difficult to take air into the lungs. Loved ones and others could watch—that was the point, after all—but they could not help the victim. Guards were posted to prevent rescue. In the end, not much was left of the victim of crucifixion. The remains would have been disposed of in summary fashion, piled with other corpses nearby, so that the dogs and ravens might finish the work already begun on the cross. This, too, was the point of crucifixion. The victim was not properly buried; his or her soul was not laid to rest. This was, to ancient sensibilities, the curse of eternal shame.

Imagining Jesus' Death

How shall we imagine the death of Jesus, taking all of this into account? It begins with a Passover pilgrim from a remote place, a nobody in the expansive Roman imperial east. But this peasant does not believe that he is a nobody. Nor will he accept this for his companions: lepers, prostitutes, outcasts, tanners, weavers, fishers. He goes to the Temple, as all others do.[7] But he is moved to anger by the scene there. What combination of emotions might have stirred him is impossible to know. As a Jew it was the center of his piety, the locus of God's sojourning with his people. Yet its keepers were also closely allied with Roman power, appointed by the Roman prefect in Caesarea, co-opted. Here is where his expendability to the larger Roman world began. So he is angry. Perhaps he does something to disrupt activity around the Temple. Perhaps he just says the wrong thing in the wrong place at the wrong time. It *is* during Passover, after all. Any small thing would be enough. If there is a trial, it does not last long. He is a peasant, a nobody. The whole world is not watching. How many would even have noticed his disappearance? If Jesus speaks, as he has done on many occasions before, of another kingdom, another empire, God's empire, the charge of sedition is secured. Why, after all, speak of another empire, an empire as God would have it, if there is not something wrong with *the* empire. And so he is crucified, not alone, but with others—probably more than two. In truth, he was crucified with thousands. If he died quickly, we should imagine him being tortured severely before he ever gets crucified. On the cross he dies of shock, or perhaps suffocation. In the end, it would not be customary for friends to take away the body. John Dominic Crossan has suggested that his body likely ended up on a pile of corpses, carrion for the dogs and the birds.[8]

I must admit that when I first read this in Crossan's book I was shocked. But in his description of the death of Jesus he had done something that all the tradition and piety of my religious training had rendered impossible through the years: he had made the death of Jesus real for me. Death—violent death—*is* a shocking thing. The image of Jesus' body lying on a pile of corpses, festering, swarmed by flies, and torn at by ravenous dogs knocked the wind out of me. It stunned me. Then I knew, for the first time, something of how those who followed him must have experienced this event. It was violent and terrifying, filled with agony and grief.

How does one find meaning in a death so violent and repulsive, so wrenching and depressing? This was the challenge faced by Jesus' first followers. No doubt, many of those who were with him disappeared back into the crowd after this. The terror of the cross had done its work. But some did not disappear. They did not give up. They got through the tragedy and horror of the moment, and then began to consider it. They considered it in light of all Jesus had meant to them, in light of the Jewish tradition, and in light of what they were beginning to experience again. Jesus had been killed, but his spirit was not dead yet. The tragedy of Jesus' death was not the final word. Words began to transform it into something else altogether: something definitive for who they would become; something that would give purpose to their lives; something that would redeem them from despair. The death of a nobody was not nothing after all.

Victim

Whatever the personal aspirations and hopes of Jesus were,
his message of the coming of God's kingdom did not leave him
as the victor, but as the victim.
—Helmut Koester, "Jesus the Victim" (1992)

Jesus, the Victim of Empire

Jesus was born into an age of peace and security such as the world had never known. It was the age of Augustus—the Augustan renaissance. The hoped-for time of peace and prosperity had finally arrived. Horace, the best-known poet of this age, proclaimed its arrival in idyllic verse:

> In safety range the cattle o'er the mead:
> Sweet Peace, soft Plenty, swell the golden grain:
> O'er unvex'd seas the sailors blithely speed:
> Fair Honour shrinks from stain:
>
> No guilty lusts the shrine of home defile:
> Cleansed is the hand without, the heart within:
> The father's features in his children smile
> Swift vengeance follows sin.
>
> Who fears the Parthian or the Scythian horde,
> Or the rank growth that German forests yield,
> While Caesar lives, who trembles at the sword
> The fierce Iberians wield?

> In his own hills each labours down the day,
> Teaching the vine to clasp the widow'd tree:
> Then to his cups again, where, feasting gay,
> He hails his god in thee. (*Odes* 4.5; LCL)

Peace, prosperity, purity, law and order—these were the watchwords of the Augustan renaissance. Jesus was born into this time. But he did not thrive in it. To the contrary, he ran afoul of this pure and virtuous age, and in the end, became its victim. How could this be?

How and why Jesus became the victim of the Roman Empire was one of the first things his followers had to come to grips with in the wake of his tragic death. This fact would shape the community of his followers in a profound way: it meant that they could never see themselves at peace with the empire and its lord. The movement that Jesus created would declare its loyalty to another Lord and another empire, and it would place at its center the things that placed Jesus at odds with *the* empire. It would become a community that was profoundly countercultural.

To understand how Jesus' death as a victim of Rome became meaningful to his followers, we might try first to understand the Roman Empire and how Jesus' words and deeds brought him into conflict with it. His crucifixion was no accident. It was meant to serve notice to anyone who would follow him that the penalty for such ideas and activity would be humiliation and agonizing death. So what was the problem with Jesus? Or, rather, what was it about the Roman imperial age that put Jesus on a collision course with those who were its guardians?

The *Pax Romana*

Romans liked to speak of their spreading domain as a great *pax*, or "peace"—the *Pax Romana*.[1] But it was a peace established and maintained through violence and intimidation. Augustus Caesar, the chief architect of the great Roman *Pax*, boasted at the end of his life that he had "brought the whole world under the empire of the Roman people."[2] Indeed, he had. Spain, Gaul, the region of the Alps, Germany, Greece, Asia Minor, Persia, the Middle East, Egypt, Ethiopia, North Africa—all lay under Roman imperial control by the end of his reign in 14 C.E. This great expansion was accomplished by the relentless waging of war. So fearsome were Rome's legions that many kings and peoples simply requested annexation to the empire, rather than face the onslaught of Caesar's troops. They knew that resistance was futile. Those who dared try were simply exterminated or enslaved. The Roman *Pax* was anything but peaceful in coming.

Palestine itself provides an excellent illustration of how one of Rome's provinces would have experienced the *Pax Romana*. On the surface, Rome's relationship to Judea and its surrounds might have appeared quite amicable. For the first century of Roman domination, Judea still had its king, its temple, and its high priests. This was not unusual in the empire. It was customary for Rome to rule its provinces through local client kings, who could take advantage of local structures and institutions—like the Jerusalem Temple—to establish imperial authority and ultimately to collect the tribute. So it was with the Jewish king, Herod the Great, established in his rule initially by Marc Anthony, and later by Augustus himself. Herod did his job well, keeping the peace on behalf of Rome. The Jewish historian Josephus describes how:

> No meeting of citizens was permitted, nor were walking together or being together permitted, and all their movements were observed. Those who were caught were punished severely, and many were taken, either openly or secretly, to the fortress of Hyrcania and there put to death. Both in the city and on the open roads there were men who spied on those who met together. And they say that even Herod himself did not neglect to play a part in this, but would often put on the dress of a private citizen and mingle with the crowds by night, and so get an idea of how they felt about his rule. Those who obstinately refused to go along with his (new) practices he persecuted in all kinds of ways. As for the rest of the populace, he demanded that

they submit to taking an oath of loyalty, and he compelled them to make a sworn declaration that they would remain friendly to his rule. Now most of the people yielded to his demand out of complaisance or fear, but those who showed some spirit and objected to compulsion he got rid of by every possible means. (*Ant.* 15.366-69; LCL)

Herod's methods were brutal, but probably typical for the more remote corners of the empire. When he died in 4 B.C.E., there was naturally hope that his successor might prove less repressive. But Rome was not interested in humanitarian ideals—at least not when it came to administering its provincial districts. Herod had requested that after his death his kingdom be divided up among his incompetent and cruel sons. When Augustus confirmed this wish, the land erupted into protest. Rome was swift in meeting this challenge to its benevolent *Pax*. Varus, the Roman governor of Syria, moved in quickly with his legions and sent his general, Gaius, into Galilee and Samaria to destroy the major centers of resistance. Among them was Sepphoris, just over the hill from Jesus' Nazareth. According to Josephus, Gaius razed the city and enslaved its inhabitants. Afterward, Varus sent his troops out to scour the hills and countryside for those who had participated in the rebellion. He rounded up two thousand of its alleged leaders and had them crucified.[3] Such was the *Pax Romana* as a young Jesus might have experienced it.

But the legions alone could not hold together so vast an empire as the Romans had acquired by the beginning of the common era. The Roman Empire was spread onto three continents, encompassing peoples as diverse as Ethiopians in the south, Britons in the north, Gauls in the west, and Persians in the east. As large and powerful as their legions were, no military force could bind together these disparate lands. So how did they do it? Two enormous powers combined to make the empire possible, one structural (or sociological), the other ideological (or theological).

The Power of Patronage

The structure of the Roman Empire is a little difficult for moderns to understand. This is because modern, postindustrial society is structured more or less into horizontal layers, each layer comprising a "class" of persons: lower class, middle class, upper class, and so on. This was not true of preindustrial agrarian empires, like Rome. In the Roman Empire the lines of division were not horizontal, but vertical, or rather, the sloping pyramidal lines of patronage. Rome was not the industrial center of a large working-class culture. It was the home of influential persons—patrons—whose power and influence spread out through the empire like large slices of pie, economic pie. To get a piece of the pie, it was necessary to be taken up into one of those informal yet powerful spheres of influence that began in Rome, but extended on out into the furthest reaches of the empire, controlling every aspect of economic and political life.

What is patronage and how did it work? A patron is a person of considerable means, acquired through economic achievement, military prowess, or (most importantly) through birth. To hold on to the power that goes with his or her position, the patron must use it to the advantage of others, who come to be seen as the patron's "clients." He or she supports these clients, giving them access to the economic or political power he or she controls. For their part, the clients support their patron from below, working on behalf of his or her interests. These clients may, in turn, serve as patrons to others located below them in the social food chain, who become their clients. Thus the network widens to include more and more persons locked into patron-client relationships. This network of patronage becomes a kind of pyramid of dependency, strongly hierarchical in nature, with the means to life flowing up and down as persons meet their obligations and receive their rewards.[4]

Within the empire there were many such pyramids extending out from Rome, each related to an important person in the Roman hierarchy. As the drama of social and economic life unfolded, patrons and their clients competed for advantage in the drive to control more and more of the means to life. Thus loyalty became a crucial value in the success of a patron and his or her clients. Loyalty could be found most readily within a family, and so families and strong family ties became important in the empire. At the top of a patronal pyramid might be a prominent Roman family, a father and his sons, a tight inner circle of patrons and clients. But also at the bottom of the pyramid, where loyalty was no less important, families were held together by their relationship to a father, who might be the client of someone higher up in the pyramid. Indeed, Romans often came to think of an entire network of patron-client relations as a giant extended family.

One can now see how the empire could be held together once the legions had withdrawn. If one wished to get along successfully in the new social order, one needed to be connected. This was a feudal society, organized not horizontally but vertically, with all the lifelines of loyalty reaching ultimately to Rome itself. At the head of all these lines was the emperor. Augustus was the patron of the whole empire. In a sense, the empire was his to do with as he pleased. He held it through the power of his clients, whose own power came from their clients, who in turn had clients of their own, and so on down through the various pyramids of patronage into each and every family in every province of the empire. Augustus understood all of this very well. Thus he encouraged and celebrated precisely those values that were key to the success of patronage: *fides, pietas, familia*—loyalty, piety, and Roman family values.

Rome's Golden Age

The second great power binding the empire together was ideological, or better, theological. The spirit of these times for Romans was deeply religious. The *Pax Romana*, for them, was no ordinary time. It was the golden age foreseen in ages past as that great time of blessing and peace foreordained by the gods and destined to descend once again upon the gods' chosen people. The Roman peace was not a secular accomplishment: it was the gift of the gods. It was a reward for virtuous living. "Thy age, great Caesar, has restored to squalid fields the plenteous grain . . . , wild passion's erring walk controll'd, heal'd the foul plague-spot of the state, and brought again the life of old" (Horace, *Odes* 4.15, LCL).

At the center of this new and glorious age was Augustus himself. It was he who established the peace, he who secured the borders, he who added province after province to the greater glory and enrichment of Rome. Moreover, it was he who, personally, carried the favor of the gods. He became in the popular imagination nothing less than a messenger from the gods—God's own son. "Behold, at last, that man, for this is he, so oft unto thy listening ears foretold, Augustus Caesar, kindred unto Jove. He brings a golden age; he shall restore old Saturn's sceptre to our Latin land"—so prophesies Virgil's ghost of Anchises in the *Aenead* (6.756, LCL).

Augustus understood this ideology and the pious feelings that fueled it. Although Roman tradition discouraged him from promoting the idea that he was in truth divine, he bathed himself in nostalgic religious ideas and ceremony. He wanted to create the impression that the gods had indeed smiled upon Rome, and that he, the *Pontifex Maximus*—the high priest of the Roman people—was responsible for calling forth this blessing. So in 17 B.C.E. he revived the ancient custom of the Secular Games, a periodic celebration intended to mark the turning of the ages. It was a kind of national week of repentance and thanksgiving, with public sacrifices, prayers, processions, and pageantry, all done with great extravagance and marvelous entertainment value. It was a religio-political event celebrating the goodness and virtue of the Roman people and their leader, the high priest, Augustus Caesar. Horace composed a hymn for the occasion, to be sung by a choir of "chosen maidens and spotless youths." This excerpt captures the spirit of the celebration:

> If Rome be your handiwork . . . , then, O gods, make teachable your youth and grant them virtuous ways; to the aged give tranquil peace; and to the race of Romulus, riches and offspring and every glory.

And whatever the glorious scion of Anchises and of Venus [Augustus], with sacrifice of milk-white steers, asks of you, that may he obtain, triumphant over the warring foe, but generous to the fallen. . . . Already Faith, Peace, Honor and ancient Modesty, and neglected Virtue have courage to return, and blessed Plenty with her full horn is seen. (Horace, *Carmen Saeculare* 37, 45-48. 49-52, 57-60; LCL)

Thus Augustus became the champion of ancient piety and traditional values: faith, peace, honor and shame, and good old-fashioned virtue. These were the building blocks of a strong society, Augustus believed. And Romans believed that he embodied these values in their purest form. The empire was to them no accident. It was their destiny, guaranteed by the piety and reverence of their political and spiritual leader, Augustus.

This pious fervor was not confined to the hills and altars of Rome itself. Indeed, one could find its strongest expression in the provinces, where local leaders, connected to Rome through the web of patronage, competed to demonstrate their loyalty to Augustus and the empire through their own extravagant displays of piety.[5] Provincial assemblies were created to promote and maintain the imperial cult. Throughout the empire one can still find its remnants today: temples in virtually every city dedicated to the gods, Roma and Augustus. Time itself was made to pay him due homage. In the province of Asia (Asia Minor) the assembled representatives of the Greek cities voted that the celebration of the New Year be shifted so that it would fall on September 23, Augustus's birthday.[6] Back home in Rome, Augustus allowed the Senate to honor him by changing the name of the eighth month from the traditional "Sextilis" to "August," a remnant of the *Pax Romana* that remains with us still.[7] From one end of the Mediterranean to the other, people were swept up into the religious and political ideology that surrounded Rome and its divine son, Augustus.

Another Empire, Another God

Jesus was born into an eastern province of Rome's vast empire during this golden age of Augustus. There, too, in Judea the cult of the emperor and the theology of empire were as strong as anywhere. Their chief promoter was Herod the Great. He was a client of Augustus himself, and he did his patron proud. Between 22 and 10 B.C.E. he built a lavish city on the Mediterranean Sea and created a harbor large enough to rival the great seaport of Alexandria in Egypt. The harbor he named "Sebaste," Greek for Augustus. The city he named Caesarea. In its center stood an enormous temple dedicated to the gods Roma and Augustus.[8] Though Jerusalem was the traditional seat of authority in Judea, the Roman governor resided in Caesarea. From here outward the patronal tentacles of the empire extended into the land—south to the cities of Sebaste, Neapolis, and Jerusalem, east to Scythopolis, and north to Sepphoris and Tiberias. All of these were cities with Gentile populations with strong Roman loyalties. The *Pax Romana* extended even to this remote land. Jesus would have grown up with it on his doorstep.

But what would it have meant for someone like him? Where did he and his family fit in Rome's imperial plan? Jesus was a carpenter, or more generally, an artisan (*tektōn*), or so tradition tells us (Mark 6:3).[9] In an agrarian empire, to be called a mere artisan is no compliment, for economic life is rooted in the land. To be part of things at all one must at least be connected to the land through agriculture. A carpenter—or any artisan or laborer, like a fisherman—was not. It is quite possible that the family of Jesus had fallen out of the mainstream.[10] Perhaps they had lost their land, as many had, during this time of Roman economic expansion and increased agricultural commercialization, or under the weight of the burdensome taxes, or tribute, paid to Rome, directly or through its vassals, the Herodians.[11] Philo, who wrote about Jewish peasant life in Roman Egypt at about this same time, gives a vivid picture of how such a thing could, and did, happen. His account is of how a certain man, appointed to collect the tribute, went about collecting from peasants in arrears on their payments:

When some of his debtors whose default was clearly due to their poverty took flight in fear of the fatal consequences of his vengeance, he carried off by force their women and children and parents and their other relatives and beat and subjected them to every kind of outrage and contumely in order to make them either tell him of the whereabouts of the fugitive or discharge their debt themselves. . . . And where there were no relatives left, the maltreatment was passed on to their neighbors and sometimes even to villages and cities which quickly became desolate and stripped of their inhabitants who left their homes and dispersed to places where they expected to remain unobserved. (Philo, *Special Laws* 3.159, 162; LCL)

For those who were part of the empire, part of its systems of patronage, of collection and distribution, the *Pax Romana* might have offered at least some level of "peace." But for those who were not, life was anything but peaceful. Jesus and his family were not part of the empire. They lived on its margins, piecing together a subsistence living by working with their hands. In his company we find other such folk, similarly marginal to the empire: fishermen, prostitutes, lepers, beggars, persons disabled by life, the demon-possessed. None of these folk would have made good clients. They belonged to that category of persons the anthropologist Gerhard Lenski calls "expendables."[12]

Being expendable to the empire was in itself no crime. An expendable is an irrelevance. But Jesus turned out to be no ordinary expendable. He took cognizance of his situation and began to reflect on it. He began to speak of another empire, an empire for all the beggars, the hungry, the depressed, and the persecuted in his world (Luke 6:20b-23//Matt 5:3, 6, 4, 11-12 [Q]; *Gos. Thom.* 54; 69:2; 68). He began to speak of a new future, in which those who are first in the present order of things would be last, and the last would be first (Mark 10:31; Luke 13:30//Matt 20:16 [Q]; *Gos. Thom.* 4:2a). He also spoke of himself as one who would bring not peace but a sword (Luke 12:51//Matt 10:34 [Q]; *Gos. Thom.* 16). He spoke of this new empire in ideal, utopian terms as God's empire.[13] But it was not an empire whose reality was never to be known in the here and now. To the contrary, it is already spread out upon the earth; people just do not see it yet (Luke 17:20-21; *Gos. Thom.* 3; 113).

This sort of talk *was* a crime. Why, after all, speak of another empire, an empire that would truly be "of God," if there is nothing wrong with the empire bestowed by the gods through the auspices of the divine Caesar, Augustus? Here was an expendable who contemplated his situation and that of those around him, and dared to imagine a new world in which he and his were not expendable after all.

They were expendable to the empire, of course, because they had nothing to offer anyone who might see them as clients. What does a beggar have to offer a patron? Nothing. But this did not matter to Jesus. He was beginning to imagine life lived outside the realm of patron-client relations. He encouraged his mendicant followers to approach a house not as a beggar but as a bearer of the empire of God. They were to offer to those they meet care for their sick, and receive from them the gift of hospitality, he counseled (Luke 10:4-9//Matt 10:7-14 [Q]; *Gos. Thom.* 14:4). John Dominic Crossan has argued that this idea—that mutual care, nourishment, and support could deliver the means to life—was at the heart of Jesus' notion of an empire of God.[14] God has provided all that people need to live; if folk would only pursue the empire of God, all that is needed would fall into place (Luke 12:22-31//Matt 6:25-33 [Q]; *Gos. Thom.* 36). There is but one patron, whose gifts are meant for all, and that is God.

In a story he used to illustrate the nature and character of the empire of God, Jesus invoked a traditional Jewish symbol of God's future reign—the heavenly banquet. But unlike the banquets a patron might throw for his many clients, the table of God is open to all, regardless of one's loyalties:

> Someone gave a great dinner and invited many. At the time for the dinner he sent his slave to say to those who had been invited, "Come, for everything is ready now." But they all alike began to make excuses. The first said to him, "I have bought a piece of land, and I must go out and see it; please accept my regrets." Another said, "I have bought five yoke of oxen, and I am going to

> try them out; please accept my regrets." Another said, "I have just
> been married, and therefore I cannot come." So the slave
> reported this to his master. . . . Then the master said to the slave,
> "Go out into the roads and lanes, and compel people to come in,
> so that my house may be filled. (Luke 14:16-24, alt.; cf. Matt 22:2-
> 13 [Q]; *Gos. Thom.* 64)

Here a patron prepares a feast for his clients, but they insult his hospitality. Their relationship, it turns out, was a sham. But never mind.
There is another way to celebrate, another way to create community.
Open the table. Anyone can come. If God is the only real patron, then
who can be denied?

Jesus began to reimagine the very basis for the patronage system,
even the family itself. He once said something like this: "Whoever
does not hate his father and his mother cannot become a disciple of
mine. And whoever does not hate his brothers and sisters (and) will
not take up his cross as I do, will not be worthy of me" (*Gos. Thom.* 55;
cf. Luke 14:26//Matt 10:37 [Q]; *Gos. Thom.* 101:1-2). On another occasion, when his mother and brothers had come to see him, he said,
"Who are my mother and my brothers . . . ? Here are my mother and
my brothers! Whoever does the will of God is my brother, and sister,
and mother" (Mark 3:35; cf. *Gos. Thom.* 99:2).

These difficult sayings are best understood when placed within the
context of a feudal patronage system, in which the family plays a fundamental role in the distribution of what the empire has to offer.
Recall that Augustus had espoused Roman family values more than
anyone before or since. Why? Family loyalty was the linchpin of the
entire system of patronage that held the empire together. Jesus pulled
that pin, creating a new family with new loyalties. Their faith (*fides*)
was directed to another empire, another God.

God and Caesar

What about the tribute? Here was the heart of the matter. After all, the
entire system of patronage and brokerage was designed to insure the

smooth flow of tribute to Rome and its selective redistribution to those whose loyalty could be trusted. Jesus was not foolhardy. He would have approached this question with great care, and perhaps cleverness. Mark includes a story about how Jesus was once approached by his opponents, who directly posed to him the question of the tribute, "'Should we pay it or not?'" Jesus replied, "'Bring me a denarius and let me see it.' And they brought one. Then he said to them, 'Whose head is this, and whose title?' They answered, 'The emperor's.' Jesus said to them, 'Give to the emperor the things that are the emperor's, and to God the things that are God's'" (Mark 12:15-17).

In modern American culture this reply has often been misunderstood as a blueprint for the separation of church and state, for dividing sacred from secular concerns. But this misses the point entirely. In Jesus' world there was no separation of church and state, sacred and secular. For Jesus, a Jew, there was *nothing* that did not belong to God.[15] "The earth is the Lord's, and the fullness thereof" (Ps 24:1). This was equally true of Romans, who thought of their expanding empire as divinely ordained, whose political leader was proclaimed the divine son of God. So what would Jesus have meant by this reply? In it he employs the skill of a clever street philosopher, constantly in danger of entrapment by his opponents. The classicists Marcel Detienne and Jean-Pierre Vernant coined a term to describe this common characteristic among the popular philosophers of the Hellenistic age: *metis*, or "cunning intelligence."[16] *Metis* is the art of the slippery reply, the clever rejoinder; it is the skill of the table-turner. The opponents of Jesus mean to trap him between the authorities on the one hand, and his tax-oppressed audience on the other. He eludes them with a reply that itself begs a question: "What *does* belong to God, and what to Caesar?" Now his opponents must reveal *their* loyalties. They are caught in their own trap. If they admit Caesar's claim, they will be stoned by the Jewish crowd; if they do not, they will be arrested. But no one in the crowd would have missed the clear subtext so elusively laid out by the unanswered question in Jesus' reply: God and Caesar are not the same, and one must choose between them.[17]

Casting out Legion

One of the things that put Jesus at odds with the empire was the apparent fact that he was an exorcist. He came from a traditional culture, in which belief in demons and spirits was common. Jesus shared this belief. In such cultures, there are people who have the ability to cast out (what are thought to be) demons. Jesus was such a person. Marcus Borg has called him a "spirit person" or "spirit-filled person."[18] In more technical terms we might call him a "shaman." The opponents of Christianity called him a *goēs*, or sorcerer—that is, an illicit holy man. This in itself made him "an enemy of the Roman people."[19] Why?

We might approach this question by looking at traditional cultures and their experience of spirit possession today. One very interesting study is I. M. Lewis's *Ecstatic Religion*.[20] Lewis noticed that in cultures where belief in spirits is common, people with little power, marginal people, or people suffering victimization in various social and political situations may become possessed by powerful spirits, which manifest themselves in outbursts of anger and frustration, harming themselves and others. Or sometimes the demon might even take on the characteristics of the victim's tormentor, now tormenting the victim in a very public way. Spirit possession may thus be a particularly powerful way of dramatizing to others one's personal sense of oppression when interpersonal or societal forces would make this otherwise impossible. Eventually an exorcist must be called in to attack the demon, and free its victim from its evil powers. Of course, in exorcising the demon he or she is at the same time symbolically taking on the power of the oblique oppressor as well. This makes the local holy man or witch a powerful mediator of cultural critique. This may be the reason why such figures are frequently marginal, or even illegal.

What sort of demonic forces might have bubbled forth as spirit possession in Roman-occupied Palestine, and what would it have meant for Jesus to confront those forces with the power to exorcise these unclean spirits? There is one story about Jesus' activity as an exorcist that certainly would have set Roman teeth on edge. The story is, in part, legend, but it looks so much like the scenarios for possession Lewis described, it might well be based in some distant historical memory. As told in the Gospel of Mark (5:1-20), Jesus encounters a demon-possessed man in the country of the Gerasenes. The man lives among the tombs, constantly howling and bruising himself with stones. Try as they might, the Gerasenes cannot subdue him. So he lives among the dead, a public spectacle of torment. When he sees Jesus, he runs to meet him, falls down in front of him, and begins to shout: "'What have you to do with me, Jesus, son of the most high God? I adjure you by God, do not torment me.' For he had said to him, 'Come out of the man, you unclean spirit.' Then Jesus asked him, 'What is your name?' He replied, 'My name is Legion; for we are many'" (Mark 5:7-9).

A demon named Legion. Imagine that, in a province that Rome more than once subdued by its legions, a province always standing under the threat of further violence should the Jews begin to chafe too severely under the burden of empire and rise up once again. Crossan is quite right in reading this story in light of Lewis's study of spirit possession.[21] Spirit possession—as with oppression, violence, and frustration—is not always strictly personal; it may also bear political markings. Crossan offers by way of analogy the remarkable example of the Lunda-Luvale tribes of the Barotse people of the former Rhodesia, studied by Barrie Reynolds in the 1960s, who, under European rule, began to experience spirit possession of a sharply political nature: "They always had . . . traditional ailments called *mahamba*, which resulted from possession by ancestral spirits. But they then developed a special modern version called *bindele*, the Luvale word for 'European,' which necessitated a special exorcistic church and a lengthy curative process for its healing."[22] Crossan summarizes the phenomenological connection clearly made across centuries and cultures: "*Legion*, I think, is to colonial Roman Palestine as *bindele* was to colonial European Rhodesia, and in both cases colonial exploitation is incarnated individually as demonic possession."[23]

Torment can come from many sources. The Gerasene demoniac bears in his body the torment and suffering of a subjugated people. Jesus responds with poetic daring, according to Mark: "Now there on the hillside a great herd of swine was feeding; and the unclean spirits begged him, 'Send us into the swine; let us enter them.' So he gave them permission. And the unclean spirits came out and entered the swine; and the herd, numbering about two thousand, rushed down the steep bank into the sea, and were drowned in the sea" (Mark 5:11-13).

In a Jewish context, this ending is none too subtle. Legion finds a fate that is doubly fitting of Rome's occupying forces: into the unclean swine, and then into the watery deep for their ultimate destruction. Jesus displays his holy powers in a conflict with the demonic Roman presence and wins. In Mark's story the Gerasenes, when they find out what has happened, beg Jesus to leave the area. An exorcist can get one into a lot of trouble.

On to the Temple

Imagine a person like Jesus in Jerusalem at Passover. Passover was the annual Jewish celebration of liberation, the commemoration of the end of Egyptian captivity. Rome understood how this festival in particular could be construed in the Roman province of Judea. The Roman prefect would have come from his normal seat in Caesarea Maritima to be present, as during all high holidays, and to make sure that the celebration remained focused on the past, not the present or future. Passover must have been a time of particularly great tension.

The Jewish historian Josephus relates an incident that illustrates how on-edge things could get during this most sensitive of times. The setting is a Passover celebration during the prefecture of Cumanus, who governed Palestine in 48–52 C.E. The scene is the Temple courtyard, an area surrounding the Temple, enclosed by a portico. A large Jewish crowd mingles in the courtyard, while Roman soldiers stand atop the portico watching for potential trouble.

"Thereupon one of the soldiers, raising his robe, stooped in an indecent attitude, so as to turn his backside to the Jews, and made a noise in keeping with his posture" (*War* 2.225; LCL). This, of course, enrages the crowd, which begins a chant for Cumanus to punish the soldier for his vulgarity. Some in the crowd begin to hurl stones up at the soldiers; fights break out. Fearing an all-out riot, Cumanus calls for more troops, who pour into the colonnades surrounding the courtyard and begin driving the people out the narrow gates. Josephus continues: "But such violence was used as they pressed round the exits that they were trodden under foot and crushed to death by one another; upwards of thirty thousand perished, and the feast was turned into mourning for the whole nation and for every household into lamentation" (*War* 2.227; LCL).

Imagine Jesus walking into that kind of tense situation. Imagine him speaking then, as he had so many times before, of a new empire, an empire of God in which the first will be last and the last first. And imagine the talk *about* him, how he cast out "Legion" in Gerasa, or how he had said that Caesar could not have what was rightly to be given only to God. Or simply imagine how a pious Jew would have felt walking into the locus of God's presence in Israel, the holy Temple of Jerusalem, and finding it policed by Roman troops looking on from the nearby fortress of Antonia, or perhaps watching from atop the Temple colonnades. Imagine how such a person as Jesus might have felt as he realized that the priests there were not troubled by this; they were part of it, woven firmly into the web of Roman imperial patronage. The high priesthood was at the time a matter of Roman appointment. Imagine how he might have felt as he was taken up into the mood of the crowd and felt the tension building around him and within him.

These are things about that final day in Jerusalem that we, of course, can never know. But we can imagine. We can imagine, as the Gospel writers did, how Jesus might have fallen into a rage and tried to disrupt activity in the Temple courtyard. We might even imagine him, as Mark does, spewing out prophetic contempt with words echoing Isaiah and

Jeremiah, "My house shall be called a house of prayer for all the nations, but you have made it a den of robbers" (Mark 12:17). If he had used these words, he would not likely have been referring to any petty thievery on the part of people selling doves and exchanging money in the porticoes. This word, *lēstēs* ("robber"), can mean much more than petty thief. A *lēstēs* is a marauder, a lawless pillager and bully who rides into town and takes what he wants. Jesus' words would have been aimed at the whole Temple apparatus in its incongruous role of arbiter of imperial power. Perhaps he even spoke of destroying the Temple (see Mark 14:58; John 2:19; *Gos. Thom.* 71). But this would not have been heard as a critique of the Jewish religion, or as an attempt to reform Judaism. It would have been heard as an indictment of the religion and politics of empire as it manifested itself in its peculiar Palestinian form: the Jerusalem Temple. If any of this took place, it would be difficult to imagine how Jesus ever could have walked out of that courtyard alive. His miraculous escape is perhaps the most fantastic part of the story, which many scholars believe is at least rooted in some historical episode.[24] In any event, Jesus did not live long after visiting the Temple. He was arrested. His trial would have been brief, if a trial was held at all. He was, after all, a mere carpenter, a nobody, an expendable. He was an expendable who cried out against the empire to which he meant nothing. Now he did mean something, however briefly, and so he was crucified. Jesus became the victim of the empire, an example to anyone else who might dare to imagine another empire under another God.

Another Age, Another Son of God

The death of Jesus, the victim of Rome's all-encompassing imperial claim, was not without meaning to those who followed him. They understood the challenge he was making to the empire and its worldview. They understood his invitation to see the world differently, to imagine another kind of imperial order, in which the first would be last and the last first, in which beggars, the hungry, the depressed, and the persecuted would have a place, in which those expendable to the empire would find their true value as children of God. That is, they understood why he was killed. His was a countercultural voice in a culture that did not tolerate dissent. When they decided to continue on with what Jesus had started, they knew that they were deciding once and for all to turn themselves against the imperial culture that surrounded them. Rome's golden age would not be their time; they imagined another future. Rome's chosen son would not be their savior; they proclaimed another Son of God.

This dissident mood pervades the literature of earliest Christianity, though it is often missed when read outside the cultural context of the Roman Empire. Take, for example, the Gospel of Mark. It begins with the line, "The beginning of the good news of Jesus Christ, the Son of God." This seems harmless enough. But if one were to have read this, say, in western Asia Minor, in the city of Priene, one would have walked each day past an inscription commemorating the introduction of the Julian calendar, which contained these words: "whereas the birthday of the god [Augustus] marked for the world the beginning of the good news, through his coming . . . ; therefore—may Good Fortune and Safety attend—it has been decreed by the Greeks in the province of Asia that the New Year shall begin in all the cities on September 23, which is the birthday of Augustus."[25] For earliest Christians, Augustus was not "the beginning of the good news." Mark understood this clearly, and so began his story with a counterclaim. His story is of another Son of God; his "good news" begins not with Rome's favorite son, but with Rome's victim—the one for whom there is a Roman cross waiting at the end of his story.

The Scum of the Earth

One sees this countercultural spirit especially in the writings of the apostle Paul. Though Paul had never known Jesus personally, he certainly picked up from his followers this dissident stance. Paul's career was marked by a constant struggle with Roman authorities: in and out of Roman jails, tortured, and—if legend preserves a kernel of truth—finally executed in Rome under the emperor Nero. Luke was not ill informed when he imagined the sort of accusations that would have been leveled against Paul and his companions as they attempted to bring their alternative "good news" to a place like Thessalonica, a major center of the imperial cult: "These people who have been turning the world upside down have come here also. . . . They are all acting contrary to the decrees of Caesar, saying that there is another emperor named Jesus" (Acts 17:6-7, alt.).

When Paul came to experience Jesus as his Lord, he also came to the realization that the *Pax Romana* was not a peace he could embrace. In Thessalonica, as elsewhere, his experience as a dissident in the empire was anything but peaceful (1 Thess 2:1-2). Later, when the Thessalonian church Paul left behind continued to experience harassment and trouble (1 Thess 3:1-5), Paul would encourage them by mocking the idea that Rome's program of *pax et securitas* was in truth peace and security after all: "When they say, 'There is peace and security,' then suddenly destruction will come upon them, as labor pains come upon a pregnant woman, and there will be no escape!" (1 Thess 5:3). As Dieter Georgi has persuasively argued, "peace and security" here is an "ironic allusion to the official theology and propaganda of the *Pax Romana*."[26] Later in this letter, Paul would share with the Thessalonian church his own apocalyptic vision of a future new age, when Jesus, himself a victim of Rome's peace, would return in a triumphal procession, "with a cry and command, with the archangel's call and with the sound of God's trumpet" (4:16), whereupon those who are left will go out "to meet the Lord" (4:17). The model for this scene, according to Georgi, is the ancient Near Eastern "legitimizing ceremony," whereby citizens go out to meet a visiting dignitary and escort him in through the gates of their city.[27] The ceremonious arrival of the emperor or his ambassadors must have been a familiar sight in a city like Thessalonica. But Paul does indeed have another "Lord" in mind. This procession is not for the keeper of the empire; it is for Jesus, the victim of the empire.

It was not just Rome and its emperor that Paul rejected. He rejected the values of the Augustan age itself. What his contemporaries regarded as wisdom, Paul regarded as foolishness. What the world regarded as foolish, he accepted as wise. This was the consequence of following a crucified Messiah. In his letter to the Corinthian churches known as First Corinthians, he writes: "Where is the one who is wise? Where is the scribe? Where is the debater of this age? Has not God made foolish the wisdom of the world? For since, in the wisdom of God, the world did not know God through wisdom, God decided, through the foolishness of our proclamation, to save those who believe. . . . We proclaim a crucified messiah, a stumbling block to Jews and foolishness to Gentiles" (1 Cor 1:20-21, 23). For Paul, following a crucified Messiah meant accepting a wisdom that was out of step with the Augustan age. Later in the same letter he continues: "Yet among the mature we do impart wisdom, although it is not a wisdom of this age or of the rulers of this age, who are doomed to pass away. . . . None of the rulers of this age understood this; for if they had, they would not have crucified the Lord of Glory" (2:6, 8).

What does it mean to follow a Messiah who was made the victim of Rome's empire? For Paul it meant seeing through what he had come to realize was a false claimant to God's hoped-for reign. The "rulers of this age" understood nothing. It meant turning one's values upside down: what seems wise is in fact foolish, and what is foolish is actually wise. It meant accepting one's fate as a fool, a person out of step with the spirit of the times. In his view, this was what some in Corinth had failed to see about following Jesus. He upbraids them, using himself as an example of one who is appropriately out of step:

> We are fools for Christ's sake, but you are wise in Christ. We are weak, but you are strong. You are held in honor, but we in disrepute. To the present hour we hunger and thirst, we are ill-clad and buffeted and homeless, and we labor, working with our own hands. When reviled, we bless; when persecuted, we endure; when slandered, we try to conciliate; we have become, and now are, as the refuse of the world, the off-scouring of all things. (4:10-13)

Here the Augustan values of strength and honor are mocked. The honorable life is not what an apostle of the crucified Messiah can rightly expect. Rather, such a person should expect the worst. The terms Paul employs in the final sentence could not be more derisive. One who follows the crucified Messiah will become the refuse of the world, regarded as filth to be thrown out with the trash. For Paul, being a loyal follower of Jesus means becoming the scum of the earth.

Life among the Scythians

This countercultural flavor was present in early Christianity for many generations—as long as Christians could still taste the humiliation of the cross, and the consequences of losing one's leader to the empire's executioner. Of course, there were also many compromises and attempts at accommodation. Paul himself, when writing to the church in Rome, would reverse his otherwise staunch stand against aligning oneself with the empire, even calling the emperor "God's servant for your good" (Rom 13:4)—if indeed Paul wrote these words.[28] One might suppose that such lapses in zeal are to be expected, especially when addressing people living in the very capital itself—in the belly of the beast. But the early church never lost the sense that Rome's empire was not really their place of peace. They looked for another day, another age to come.

Perhaps it is no accident that among the writings of the New Testament, the most stridently anti-Roman text is also the most thoroughly apocalyptic: the Apocalypse of John (Revelation).[29] John seems to have comprehended clearly that Rome and the church fostered different visions of the world's ideal future. While Rome nurtured the *Pax Romana*, John believed that true peace would come to the world only when the Roman beast was thrown into a sea of fire, never to be heard from again (Rev 19:20). Then and only then could the earth become a place fit for gods. His vision unfolds like a dream:

> Then I saw a new heaven and a new earth; for the first heaven and
> the first earth had passed away, and the sea was no more. And I
> saw the holy city, new Jerusalem, coming down out of heaven
> from God, prepared as a bride adorned for her husband; and I
> heard a loud voice from the throne saying, "Behold, the dwelling
> place of God is with humanity. He will dwell with them, and they
> shall be his people, and God himself will be with them; he will
> wipe away every tear from their eyes, and death shall be no more,
> neither shall there be mourning nor crying nor pain any more,
> for the former things have passed away." (Rev 21:1-4)

The power of these words is felt only when one successfully imagines
them on the lips of someone who had seen the inside of a Roman
prison. When John expresses his hope for deliverance from pain, tears,
and death one can be sure that this is not mere poetic fancy. He has
known pain and grief, and death surrounds him. This was the fate of
many who chose to embrace the crucified Messiah.

In fact, when we first hear of Christianity and Christians in the
wider literature of antiquity, it is to report on their illegal activity and
their arrest, torture, and execution. The report is in a letter of Pliny
the Younger, the newly appointed legate of Bithynia, to the emperor
Trajan, written in about 111 C.E.[30] Pliny had discovered in his province
a strange group of religious zealots such as he had never before
encountered. In order to find out the truth about this "depraved and
excessive superstition" he captured and tortured two slave girls said
to be "deaconesses" in the movement. Although he could find nothing particularly insidious about their activities, he nonetheless had
them executed. Their crime was not so much following Jesus—a figure
no doubt obscure and unknown to Pliny—but choosing not to worship the statue of the emperor and the images of the gods: disloy-
alty.[31] Pain, torture, and death: these were the fate of anyone who
refused to embrace the empire, and chose instead to hope for something else.

Christian resistance to Roman authority did not die out even as the
centuries wore on. In the third century we encounter it with astonish-

ing force in Origen's answer to the pagan critic of Christianity, Celsus. Celsus, writing a century before, had accused Christianity of being an illegal secret association. What is surprising about Origen's reply to this accusation is that he does not deny it. To the contrary, he justifies it in a most provocative way, comparing Roman authorities to the legendary savage barbarians, the Scythians:

> if a man were placed among Scythians, whose laws were unholy, and having no opportunity of escape, were compelled to live among them, such a one would with good reason, for the sake of the law of truth, which the Scythians would regard as wickedness, enter into associations contrary to their laws, with those likeminded with himself. . . . For as those persons would do well who should enter into a secret association in order to put to death a tyrant who had seized upon the liberties of the state, so Christians also, when tyrannized over by him who is called the devil, and by falsehood, form leagues contrary to the laws of the devil, against his power, and for the safety of those others whom they may succeed in persuading to revolt from a government which is, as it were, "Scythian," and despotic! (*Against Celsus* 1.1 [ANF 4.397])

Origen wrote these positively treasonous words in 248 C.E., just a year before the emperor Decius came to power and initiated the most widespread and systematic persecution of Christians that had yet been experienced in the empire. Small wonder that Origen was arrested, imprisoned, and tortured for his defiant effrontery.

Jesus the Victim

What does it mean for Christian faith that at the center of our tradition is a person whose life ended on a Roman cross, who was the victim of an imperial system that easily exploited its conquered serfs and cast off as expendable anyone who could not, or would not, contribute to the empire's greater glory? It means that Christian faith must be very suspicious of its imperial suitors, which have been many over the centuries. How easily has Christianity been co-opted by the various empires that have played host to it. How easily has the Christian agenda merged with the agenda of imperial domination, especially in the twentieth century. Can we honestly say that Jesus would have fit better amid the values and priorities of our own culture than he did in first-century Roman Palestine? Can we honestly believe that Jesus would not have ended up the victim of our culture, just as decisively as he became the victim of his own?

Recalling the earliest Christian attempt to understand the death of Jesus as the death of a victim can serve to remind those who would follow him today that this still involves embracing a vision of the future that is countercultural. Christians must still be willing to embrace ideas that will be considered foolhardy by most arbiters of culture today. Christians must still be willing to engage in cultural critique, even when such criticism might place in jeopardy one's pursuit of a successful life. North American Christians, especially, must realize that we live in the belly of the beast, in the very heart of empire. The *Pax Americana* is no less insidious and exploitative of the world's people than was the *Pax Romana*. And it is scarcely less violent with those who would challenge its authority and its vision. Recalling that Jesus was the victim of just this kind of *pax* should make us think twice if ever we are tempted to merge the *Pax Americana* and the Christian hope for the future into one glorious vision of world peace. Such a peace would not be God's peace—at least not as it appeared in the life of Jesus, the victim of the world's last great *pax*.

Jesus died the victim of an empire that is not so different from our own. If we are to take seriously the challenge that Jesus holds for human life today, we must take seriously the fact of his death. His death is not to be dismissed as meaningless, a mere prelude to greater glories to come. Jesus' death became meaningful to people, first, in its reality as the death of a victim. His death as a victim might hold meaning for us still, if we have the courage to face it—and to face the consequences of realizing how inhospitable the world remains to Jesus' vision of God's empire. We still proclaim a crucified Messiah. To proclaim the cross is to proclaim Jesus' death, his death as a victim. If we miss this harsh reality and rush immediately on to the resurrection, we risk eviscerating our faith before we ever really take to heart the challenge with which Christian faith began. It began with the death of a victim.

Martyr

*If any want to become my followers, let them deny
themselves and take up their cross and follow me.*
—Mark 8:34

To Die for a Cause

Though the followers of Jesus remained mindful that Jesus had died at the hands of the Roman Empire and its allies, they came very quickly also to understand that Jesus' death was not merely that of a victim. It had a purpose. But what was that purpose, and how was it related to the future his followers would now face without their teacher and friend? Why did Jesus die?

Those who had followed Jesus—nearly all of them Jews—were not without cultural resources for interpreting the unjust death of a righteous person. For centuries Jews had suffered under foreign rule. This was not the first time someone had suffered and died for dissenting from the version of life offered by those who ruled them. In Jesus' own day there were many who had died thus. Jesus' followers had themselves known oppression. They had seen dissidents before. They knew what a martyr was.

The Greek word *martys* means "witness." A martyr is someone whose death in the face of great opposition becomes a witness to others. The compelling thing about martyrs is their courage in remaining faithful to their principles in the face of dire threat, even to the point of death. The steadfastness of the martyr bears witness to two things. First, it testifies to the ultimate value of the cause for which the martyr was willing to give his or her life. Second, it provides an example of faithfulness for others to emulate.

A simple saying from the Gospel of Mark is supremely illustrative of martyrological thinking: "If any want to become my followers, let them deny themselves and take up their cross and follow me" (Mark 8:34). It is possible that Jesus said something like this, anticipating the trouble that he and his companions were likely to encounter. More important, though, is the interpretive value this saying came to have as Jesus' followers struggled to find meaning in his death. It expresses on the one hand his own willingness to face death, if need be, for God's new empire. On the other hand, it is an invitation to others to do likewise. His followers would now have to ask themselves: How important is this cause, really? This is the soul-searching question posed by the martyr's death.

The Death of God's Righteous One

In the period of Christian origins a number of popular stories—some of them very old—circulated among the Jews, which focused on Jewish heroes living in the court of a foreign ruler.[1] In these "court tales" the hero, caught in the web of foreign rule, must decide between bowing to the wishes of the heathen king or remaining faithful to the God of the Jews. The legends surrounding Daniel, Susanna, Esther, and the Maccabees all unfold in just this way. These great heroes of Jewish legend and lore all face great danger, torture, even death, but in the end remain faithful to God against the tyrant king.

Understandably, such stories were popular among Jews living under Roman rule. The example of their heroes was meant to inspire faithfulness and to strengthen Jews against the betrayal of their tradition. In his study of these court tales, George Nickelsburg is able to identify a set of themes, or plot, common to many of them.[2] Together they create the basis of a genre of story Nickelsburg called "The Story of the Persecution and Exaltation of the Righteous Man." In this generic storyline, the hero becomes the victim of provocation and conspiracy. Eventually he or she must decide between obedience to God and giving in to the demands of a foreign ruler. The hero trusts God, is obedient, but must as a consequence suffer persecution, slander, false accusation, trial, and ultimately condemnation. But this is not the end. The hero is rescued, redeemed, and ultimately vindicated against his or her enemies. At last the hero is exalted and made an example for all to see and—presumably—to imitate.

The pattern Nickelsburg saw was not limited to works of narrative fiction and martyrology. One finds it in the more poetic wisdom literature of the period as well. The martyrs had a lesson to teach, and it was taught in hymns, poetry, and classroom literature. One of the most compelling presentations of this idea of the suffering righteous one is found in a Jewish work from the first century B.C.E., the Wisdom of Solomon. In the following excerpt the author gives voice to the thoughts of the wicked who would oppress God's righteous one:

> Let us lie in wait for the righteous man,
> > because he is inconvenient to us and opposes our actions;
> He reproaches us for sins against the law,
> > and accuses us of sins against our training.
> He professes to have knowledge of God,
> > and calls himself a child of the Lord.
> He became to us a reproof of our thoughts;
> > the very sight of him is a burden to us,
> because his manner of life is not like that of others,
> > and his ways are strange.
> We are considered by him as something base,
> > and he avoids our ways as unclean;
> he calls the last end of the righteous happy,
> > and boasts that God is his father.
> Let us see if his words are true,
> > and let us test what will happen at the end of his life;

for if the righteous man is God's child, he will help him,
    and will deliver him from the hand of his adversaries.
Let us test him with insult and torture,
    so that we may find out how gentle he is,
    and make trial of his forbearance.
Let us condemn him to a shameful death,
    for, according to what he says, he will be protected.
                    (Wisdom of Solomon 2:12-20)

So plots the wicked against God's righteous one. But it is to no avail. In the next chapter, there is redemption:

But the souls of the righteous are in the hand of God,
    and no torment will ever touch them.
In the eyes of the foolish they seem to have died,
    and their departure was thought to be a disaster,
    and their going from us thought to be their destruction;
    but they are at peace.
For though in the sight of others they were punished,
    their hope is full of immortality.
Having been disciplined a little, they will receive great good,
    because God tested them and found them worthy of himself;
    like gold in the furnace he tried them,
    like a sacrificial burnt offering he accepted them.
In the time of their visitation they will shine forth,
    and will run like sparks through the stubble.
They will govern nations and rule over peoples,
    and the Lord will reign over them forever.
Those who trust in him will understand truth,
    and the faithful will abide with him in love,
    because grace and mercy are upon the holy ones,
    and he watches over the elect.
                    (Wisdom of Solomon 3:1-9)

When Jesus' followers first began to formulate their convictions about him in light of his death, texts and traditions such as this one became important to them. They were grounded in the peculiar Jewish prophetic tradition that finds expression in the mysterious Suffering Servant Songs of Second Isaiah,[3] but given shape and form in the real experiences of Jews living under successive foreign rulers unsympathetic to their way of life. As such they offered a powerful framework for understanding the death of Jesus on a Roman cross. Like God's righteous servant, Jesus came to be seen as the target of enemies who conspired against him. He irritated his opponents, accusing them of transgressing against the law and of hypocrisy. He claimed to know God, to be a servant of God, even "God's child." His words and deeds were an offense, his manner of life strange. He boasted that God was his father. In the end, his enemies captured him and subjected him to the most shameful death. But he was not lost, ultimately. God redeemed him, accepted him "like a sacrificial burnt offering." One day, they hoped, he would return to rule the nations of the earth. In the meantime, those who trusted in God would know the truth, and they would abide in his love.

The followers of Jesus did not arrive at these ideas from out of the blue. Nor did these ideas derive naturally from the events of Jesus' life. They were the product of thinking about his life in light of a long Jewish tradition of considering the fate of God's suffering servants, God's "righteous ones." Certain aspects of his life—his countercultural lifestyle, for example—could take on special significance and become meaningful in new ways when viewed through the lens of this tradition. His shameful death was no longer a disaster, but could be seen as the expected fate of one who remained true to God in the face of wicked adversaries. His followers could see the cross as a powerful moment of witness, but not the end of Jesus' mission. Christians could hope for a new day, when Jesus would finally be vindicated before his enemies.

The Passion Narrative and the Wisdom Tale

Among the first written attempts to account for what had happened to Jesus was the story of his final days, trial, and death, known as the Passion Narrative. This is the source that many believe was used by the writers of Mark and John, and perhaps also another fragmentary Gospel, the *Gospel of Peter*, to give account of Jesus' death.[4] Not surprisingly, when Nickelsburg looked at the Passion Narrative against the backdrop of the Wisdom Tale, he found that the parallels were extensive.[5] Indeed, he could argue that it was this old Jewish tale of suffering and vindication that gave the Passion Narrative its basic plot and structure. The chart below, adapted from Nickelsburg's study and incorporating additions from Burton Mack's similar treatment, makes it possible to see how extensive the parallels are.[6]

Stories of Persecution and Vindication and the Passion Narrative as Used by Mark (items out of sequence are in parentheses)	
Elements of Nickelsburg's Wisdom Tale	In the Passion Narrative as used by Mark
Provocation	11:15-17
Conspiracy	11:18; 14:1
Decision	14:3-9, 35-36, 41-42
Trust	14:35-36
Obedience	14:3-9, 35-36
Accusation	14:57-61
Trial	14:53-64
Condemnation	14:64
Protest	
Prayer	14:35-36
Assistance	
Ordeal	15:29-30
Reaction	(14:63)
Rescue	(14:62)
Vindication	15:38 (14:62)
Exaltation	(14:62)
Investiture	
Acclamation	15:39
Reactions	15:39
Punishment	(15:38)

Nickelsburg's quite plausible theory of how his Wisdom Tale gave rise to the story contained in the Passion Narrative serves, of course, to underscore what most modern biblical scholarship affirms, that the Gospels and their sources are not historical archives. Committing to memory the things that took place, exactly as they took place, was not the task early Christians found laid at their feet in the years following Jesus' death. What was imperative for their own survival as a community was the task of discerning meaning in the life and death of the one who had brought them together in the first place. The writer responsible for the Passion Narrative did not begin with the question, What really happened? Whether he knew the details of Jesus' final days or not, he surely knew enough: that the one in whom they had come to believe was now dead, executed in shame on a Roman cross. Beyond this, any further historical detail would be superfluous. The important question was not what really happened. The questions—the truly important questions—were now, Were we right about him or not? Were we right to follow him? Was his cause just?

The writer of the Passion Narrative had somehow answered these soul-searching questions affirmatively. He had come to believe that Jesus was not a criminal; nor was he simply a victim. He was one of God's righteous ones, who died true to his convictions. So this author composed the story of Jesus' final days as the story of God's persecuted righteous one. He filled its episodes with allusions to the several psalms that speak of God's righteous sufferer and to the Suffering Servant Songs of Second Isaiah.[7] For Christians, Jesus would become the preeminent suffering righteous one. His faithfulness and obedience would become a witness to the value of his cause, and an example for anyone willing to take up the cross as their own fate.

A Noble Death

These ideas about death and persecution were not unique to Jewish culture in the period of Christian origins. They were part of a broader cultural view of what constitutes a meaningful death in the Hellenistic world. To die nobly for a cause, to remain true to one's principles to the very end—this was a time-honored ideal in Hellenistic culture generally speaking. In this period popular philosophers extensively discussed death and how to face it with equanimity and courage without compromising one's convictions.[8]

The most illustrious example of one who had died thus was Socrates. One of the most memorable scenes in all of literature is the death of Socrates, recounted in Plato's *Phaedo*. Already condemned for impiety and corrupting the young men of Athens, Socrates is met by his disciples one last time before he must die. As they arrive at the prison, he is just being released from his chains, for this is to be the day of his execution. As they enter the prison, his beloved Xanthippe bursts into tears at the sight of them. Socrates, nobly, asks his disciple Crito to see to her needs as she is led away, baby in her arms. Now, at length he discourses with his disciples: on how to endure pain and suffering, on how to face death, and on the nature of the world. When he has finished, Crito asks: "And have you any commands for us, Socrates?" He replies: "If you take care of yourselves you will serve me and mine and yourselves, whatever you do, even if you make no promises now; but if you neglect yourselves and are not willing to live following step by step, as it were, in the path marked out by our present and past discussions, you will accomplish nothing, no matter how much or how eagerly you promise at present" (*Phaedo* 115b-c [LCL]). Here is the real focus of the martyrological tradition: "to live following step by step . . . in the path" laid down by the martyr. The martyr asks of his followers only that they live as he lived, that they embrace the values he embraced, even if it should mean death in the end. At last Socrates drinks the hemlock and dies, in peace, true to his principles to the very end.

Socrates' death was the paradigmatic noble death; he was "of all those of his time . . . the best and wisest and most righteous man," says Phaedo (118a [LCL]). "Both in his bearing and his words, he was meeting death so fearlessly and nobly. And so I thought that even in going to the abode of the dead he was not going without the protection of the gods, and that when he arrived there it would be well with him, if it ever was well with anyone. And for this reason I was not at all filled with pity, as might seem natural when I was present at a scene of mourning" (*Phaedo* 58e-59a [LCL]). Plato's masterful depiction of Socrates' death was not meant to evoke pity or regret. His death was a witness—a martyr's death. In it we are to see how one might die nobly. Indeed, says Socrates, "is not [philosophy] the practice of death?" (*Phaedo* 80e-81a [LCL]). Perhaps not always. But when convictions place one in harm's way, the philosopher's highest calling is to die nobly, true to one's principles.

At least this is how the death of Socrates was appropriated in the Hellenistic philosophical tradition. In the first century C.E. the problem of death, and how to face it with dignity, was ubiquitous in philosophical discourse. This is perhaps understandable. Rome's empire was totalitarian. It could not tolerate dissent, and the philosophers often dissented. Then, indeed, philosophy was the practice of death. Many faced the choice that Socrates had faced: to live in compromise or to die with honor. For such folk, Socrates became a martyr, a model. The first-century Cynic philosopher Epictetus writes: "Socrates does not save his life with (the) dishonor (of escaping death by compromising his principles), the man who refused to put the vote when the Athenians demanded it of him, the man who despised the tyrants, the man who held such noble discourse about virtue and moral excellence; this man it is impossible to save by dishonor, but he is saved by death, and not by flight" (*Discourses* 4.1.164-65 [LCL]). Here death is not a disaster, an ending. It is salvation. Death in this tradition is transformed from defeat into victory. In fact, a noble death may become the capstone to a well-led life, one that transforms that life and makes it ultimately more useful to others.

Epictetus continues: "If we had been useful in our way of living, would we not have been much more useful to people by dying when it was necessary and in the manner called for? And now that Socrates is dead, the memory of him is no less useful to people. In fact, it is perhaps even more useful than what he did or said while he stilled lived"

(*Discourses* 4.1.168-69 [LCL, alt.]). For Epictetus, death was not the end of Socrates and his benefits for humankind. To the contrary, his manner of death transformed him into something more than what he had been in life.

The idea of dying nobly, with unflinching bravery and loyalty, was not limited to the philosophers. It was a standard theme in stories of military heroes, or anyone who was called upon to face death with dignity. It appears again and again, for example, in the tragedies of Euripides, as the ideal way for one to face whatever the gods might ordain, including and especially death.[9] In his study of the Noble Death tradition in Hellenistic literature, David Seeley identifies five key ideas that usually appear in various discussions and depictions of the noble death of individuals whose lives are seen as exemplary:[10] (1) The one who dies nobly dies in *obedience* to his or her principles, or often, to some higher (divine) calling or mandate. (2) In doing so, the hero demonstrates how to *overcome physical vulnerability*, to face torture and death without fear. (3) The standoff with the hero frequently involves a *military setting*—loyalty is often at stake. (4) Such a death is often seen as *vicarious* for others insofar as it may be imitated. Vicariousness comes through mimesis in this tradition. (5) Finally, there are often *sacrificial overtones* as the death of the hero is described and interpreted.

This idea of the Noble Death most certainly influenced Jewish writers of this period, as may be seen especially in the martyrological literature discussed by Nickelsburg and others. Perhaps the best example is to be found in the book known as Fourth Maccabees, a Hellenistic Jewish work written in the period of Christian origins, probably in Antioch.[11] Ostensibly, the book is a defense of the idea that reason—that is, "the mind making the deliberate choice of the life of wisdom" (1:15)—can rule over the bodily passions. To prove the point, the author takes the example of an aged priest, Eleazar, seven pious brothers, and their mother, all of whom were tortured to death during the Jewish struggle for freedom against Antiochus IV Epiphanes in the second century B.C.E. In spite of their gruesome ordeal, these martyrs all remained faithful to God. Their noble deaths two centuries earlier became an inspiration for Jews living under Roman rule, who faced many of the same challenges their ancestors had faced under Antiochus.

In Fourth Maccabees one may clearly see the marks of the Noble Death tradition, as described by Seeley.[12] The story unfolds in the context of a war—thus the military setting. The overarching theme of Fourth Maccabees is, of course, obedience. As the torturer stokes the fires that will soon sear his flesh, the elderly Eleazar takes his stand: "We, Antiochus, who firmly believe that we must lead our lives in accordance with the divine law, consider that no compulsion laid on us is mighty enough to overcome our own willing obedience to the law" (4 Macc 5:16).

Eleazar may speak with such confidence because in his resolve, he has overcome the sense of physical vulnerability that might cause him, out of fear, to capitulate to the tyrant's demands. He mocks Antiochus and his threats of torture:

> I will not violate the solemn oaths of my ancestors to keep the law, not even if you gouge out my eyes and burn my entrails. I am neither so old nor short of manliness that in the matter of religion my reason should lose its youthful vigor. So set the torturer's wheel turning and fan the fire to a great blaze. I am not so sorry for my old age as to become responsible for breaking the law of my fathers. I will not play you false, O law, my teacher; I will not forswear you, beloved self-control; I will not shame you, philosophic reason, nor will I deny you, venerable priesthood and knowledge of the law. (4 Macc 5:29-36)

Thus the ordeal begins, described in graphic detail by the author for his enrapt audience. Eleazar is stripped, scourged, and abused by his torturers. His friends try to offer him a way out. "Just pretend to taste the swine's flesh," they counsel. But he refuses. The death he dies is not a private, solitary act. It is public, a witness to others. He will not "become a model of impiety to the young by setting them an example of eating unclean food." In this sense his death is vicarious, "for others": it gives others an example to emulate. "Therefore, O children of Abraham, you must die nobly for piety's sake" (4 Macc 6:22).

So the torture continues: Eleazar is branded; an "evil-smelling concoction" is poured in his nose; he is thrown into the fire itself. At last, as he is about to expire, he lifts his eyes to God and prays: "You know, O God, that though I could have saved myself I am dying in these fiery torments for the sake of the law. Be merciful to your people and let our punishment be a satisfaction on their behalf. Make my blood their purification and take my life as a ransom for theirs" (4 Macc 6:27-29). Thus Eleazar's death becomes vicarious in another way: it is a sacrifice for the purification of the land.[13]

Obedient unto Death

The idea of the Noble Death was a common one in the culture of Hellenism and in the Hellenistic Judaism that emerged in the period of Christian origins. It may have been particularly strong in the city of Antioch, the home of a shrine to the Maccabean martyrs. Antioch was also a place where Paul spent a good deal of time early in his life as a follower of Jesus. It may also have been the home of the Gospel writers responsible for the Gospel of Mark and the Gospel of John. It is therefore not at all surprising to find many of the ideas associated with martyrdom and the Noble Death tradition in the literature of early Christianity.[14] Jesus was tortured to death by an empire that Christians regarded as tyrannical. This made the tradition of the Noble Death relevant. When one examines how the death of Jesus is treated in the texts and traditions that emerge, especially from Antiochene Christian circles, one sees immediately the profound influence of the Noble Death.

Let us begin with Paul. He, more than any other early follower of Jesus, is credited with the most active and imaginative interpretive effort in presenting Jesus, the crucified Messiah, to the wider Hellenistic world. But when Paul began to develop his characteristic preaching, he did not begin from scratch. He came into the Jesus

movement relatively late, when many traditions had already been for-
mulated. Some of these traditions he would have encountered first in
Antioch.

One of the earliest pieces of Christian tradition we have is a hymn
to Christ that Paul quotes in his letter to the Philippians. It is a complex hymn, blending ideas of the Hebrew prophets, language from the
Roman imperial cult, and the mythic pattern of the descending/
ascending redeemer known from many ancient Near Eastern religions.[15] But at the very center of this hymn is a single line—perhaps
the only clearly Christian contribution to the hymn at all—in which
we find that central theme of the martyrological tradition, obedience:

> Who, though he was in the form of God,
>   did not count equality with God a thing to be grasped,
> but emptied himself, taking the form of a slave,
>   being born in human likeness,
> And being found in human form he humbled himself
>   and became *obedient unto death,* even death on a cross.
> Therefore God has highly exalted him
>   and bestowed on him the name which is above every name,
> that at the name of Jesus every knee should bow,
>   in heaven and on earth and under earth,
> and every tongue confess that Jesus Christ is Lord,
>   to the glory of God the Father. (Phil 2:6-11)

Paul dictates this traditional hymn into a letter he is writing from
a Roman prison cell, probably in Ephesus. He is in trouble, again.
This time, he does not know whether he will live or die. Now he has
received word from Philippi that the church he founded there is in
trouble too. They have sent word to him, inquiring: What does this
mean that you are in prison and we suffer here in Philippi? Perhaps
some have raised questions about his credibility. How can a true
apostle get into so much trouble (see 1:15-18)? But Paul does not see
his current troubles as a mark against him. Rather, they are his
opportunity to bear witness to the cause, their new way of life "in
Christ." Thus Paul addresses the Philippians in terms that should by

now be familiar: "I know that through your prayers and the help of the Spirit of Jesus Christ this will turn out for my deliverance, as it is my eager expectation and hope that I shall not be at all ashamed, but that with full courage now as always Christ will be honored in my body, whether by life or by death. For to me to live is Christ, and to die is gain" (1:19-21). Paul is prepared to die nobly. "I shall not be ashamed . . . , Christ will be honored in my body," he vows. And he urges the Philippians also to "stand firm," and not be frightened. It is their privilege to "suffer for his (Christ's) sake" (1:27-30). It is in the midst of this exhortation to bear up nobly for the cause of Christ that Paul includes the hymn, perhaps a hymn already familiar to the Philippians. Christ died nobly, obedient to the end. This is Paul's aim as well. As Jesus sacrificed his life for the cause of his new empire of God, so also now Paul will offer his own life for the sake of those who would be faithful to that new reality and hope. He is ready, he says, "to be poured out as a libation upon the sacrificial offering of your faith" (2:17).

This is how the martyrological tradition works. The martyr's death is vicarious insofar as it sets an example to be emulated by others.[16] Its benefits are experienced through imitation. Jesus' death became, in this tradition, the expression of obedience. He was no longer simply a victim. He died willingly, nobly, for a cause. His obedience unto death, "even death on a cross," became a model for his followers who might also find themselves imprisoned, tortured, even executed for the cause of God's new empire. Paul has taken this witness to heart. Now he offers himself as a sacrifice, obedient to the cause, even under the threat of death. He also expects that the Philippians will come to see their own suffering and threat of death in the same way. The death of Jesus has become part of the Christian way of living. This way of life always carries with it the threat of death. As Paul writes to another church—in Corinth—again, defending his record of constant trouble and conflict with the authorities: "We are afflicted in every way, but not crushed; perplexed, but not driven to despair; persecuted, but not forsaken; struck down, but not destroyed; always carrying in the body the death of Jesus, so that the life of Jesus may also be manifested in our bodies. For while we live we are always being given up to death for Jesus' sake, so that the life of Jesus may be manifested in our mortal flesh" (2 Cor 4:8-11).

Here are the themes found so prominently in the Jewish martyrological tradition, especially in 2 and 4 Maccabees, as well as in the Stoic tradition,[17] of bearing up nobly for the sake of one's principles: freedom from concern over what might happen to one's body and the consequent freedom to act in accord with one's conscience, in spite of dire threat. To be sure, Paul's perspective is unique: rather than his strength of "reason," Paul relies on the transcendent power of God working through his earthen vessel of a body to carry him through his trials. Nonetheless, the martyrological orientation of such talk is clear.

Consider Yourself Dead

While Paul used the traditions of the early Jesus movement in his preaching and writing, he was also an innovator, a creative practical theologian. The idea that Jesus' death was a vicarious death, at once his and ours, was intriguing to him. As he pondered this martyrological notion, he also had before him his own experience of Jesus as a spiritual force in his life. The spirit of Jesus, the risen Lord, had taken over Paul, such that he could say quite seriously, "It is no longer I who live, but Christ who lives in me" (Gal 2:20b). Finally, he had before him the liturgical life of the early Jesus movement, especially its practice of baptizing persons who wished to dedicate themselves to Jesus. In Paul's last known letter, to the Romans, all of these things come together in one of Paul's most elegant formulations expressing the significance of Jesus' death: Romans 6:1-11.

The issue that consumes Paul in this part of Romans is the question of sin. Recall that in Paul's version of Christianity, the Jewish law was not to be binding on the followers of Jesus. This raised a question for those who saw the law as the code by which righteousness could be distinguished from sin. In trying to live without it, was Paul not embracing a life of sin? "Are we to continue in sin that grace may abound?" he asks, rhetorically (6:1), supplying the words he imagines his critics to be thinking. To this he replies emphatically, "Not at all! How can we who died to sin still live in it? Do you not know that all of us who have been baptized into Christ Jesus were baptized into his death? We were buried therefore with him by baptism into death, so that as Christ was raised from the dead by the glory of the Father, we too might walk in newness of life" (6:2-4).

For Paul, baptism is baptism into Christ's death. What could he mean by this, and how did such an idea address the problem of sin? To understand Paul's meaning one must realize that for Paul sin is not just bad behavior. It is a cosmic power, a force loose in the universe to which we poor human beings are subject. Sin, for Paul, is the cumulative force of evil exercising power over humanity. Such an idea, foreign perhaps to moderns, was a common way of thinking in antiquity. The universe, for ancients, was full of such hostile forces against which mere mortals were powerless. Sin, as an evil power, exercised its control over a person through the flesh—the "sinful body," says Paul (6:6)—the seat of all the passions in Paul's ancient anthropology. If this was so, then ultimately a person's only escape from sin's power is death, when the body of flesh passes away. From out of this thought world Paul arrives at a new way of considering Jesus' death as a vicarious event. If Jesus' death is at once the death of anyone who would follow him, then in his death lies the key to ultimate freedom: freedom from the power of sin:

> We know that our old self was crucified with him so that the sinful body might be destroyed, and we might no longer be enslaved to sin. For he who has died is freed from sin. But if we have died with Christ, we believe that we shall also live with him. For we know that Christ, being raised from the dead, will never die again; death no longer has dominion over him. The death he died he died to sin, once for all, but the life he lives he lives to God. So you also must consider yourselves dead to sin and alive to God. (6:6-11)

But how could this be? How could a person really become united with Jesus in his death? Paul decides that this is the ritual meaning of baptism. He takes a concept that had been expressed primarily in a literary mode—the vicarious death of a martyr—and gives it ritual power. He can do this because Jesus has become for him more than a martyr. He is a divine being, an epiphany, a spiritual force in his own right. Worship and ritual "work" with him: one could be united with Jesus the Christ spiritually, ritually. That Paul chooses the ritual of baptism to bear this burden of meaning is quite understandable. On the one hand, death and water were connected in various ways symbolically and mythically in antiquity. Jews had long associated ritual washing with purification from sin and ritual uncleanness. All of this must have been wrapped up together in the poetics of Paul's new formulation of the meaning of baptism.

What is most impressive about Paul's interpretive work here is the extent to which he seems to understand how ritual really works in the life of a believer. However powerful and poetically effective a ritual might be, it is not magic. Ritual can create a real experience of altered reality, an intense moment—in this case—of freedom. But when the event is over, life stands waiting outside the door, ready to reassert itself when the priests have disrobed and the ritual fires have been extinguished. Paul understands all of this very well. Consequently, he does not say that those who have died with Jesus in the act of baptism have also been raised with him. That final and permanent freedom lies still in the future.[18] Rather, Paul carefully asserts that "as Christ was raised . . . , we too might walk in newness of life" (6:4). Life is still there, waiting to be walked. Baptism has not changed that reality. We are not dead yet! So, he insists, "you also must *consider yourselves dead to sin and alive to God*" (6:11). The future of freedom remains still to be constructed. "Let not sin therefore reign in your mortal bodies, to make you obey their passions . . . , but yield yourselves to God as people who have been brought from death to life" (6:12-13).[19] So long as we still have a body, we still have before us the martyr's challenge: obedience. The death of Jesus is vicarious, for others, only insofar as they choose to embrace his death and his life as their own.

The One Who Endures to the End

This idea, drawn from the tradition of the Noble Death, that the death of the martyr could have vicarious effects for others was a powerful one. As Paul worked out its implications in ritual, others continued the literary tradition of martyrology, telling the story of Jesus in a way that invited its imitation, in life and in death. The Gospel of Mark is one result of this literary effort.[20]

The idea of Jesus the martyr had obvious relevance to the writer of this first Gospel. Mark was written during or just following the years of the Jewish War for independence from Rome (66–70 C.E.). As a messianic Jew who believed in Jesus, Mark's author would have found no comfort with Rome. But his beliefs about Jesus would have put him at odds with most Jews as well—he was a heretic at a time when solidarity and loyalty to the Jewish tradition were in high demand. He was a person caught between the two sides of a war-torn world. He was also part of a community that found itself in this precarious situation as well. He and his community had come to a moment of truth. Are we right or are we wrong? Is following Jesus worth the risk we must now take? The issue of faithfulness and loyalty runs throughout Mark's Gospel.

We have already seen how the Passion Narrative took up the question of Jesus' death, as the death of God's persecuted righteous one. Mark knew this early text. But he wanted more from his narrative than just an account of Jesus' unjust death. He wanted to create a narrative that would involve his audience, that would tie their fate together with that of Jesus. So Mark took up the Passion Narrative, but he used it to write his own story of Jesus. In it he wove the Passion Narrative into a skillful plot that focuses the martyr's question on the lives of those for whom he wrote, always asking: Can you remain faithful in the midst of adversity?

One way he does this is by creating a narrative pattern to which Norman Perrin called attention some years ago.[21] Perrin noticed that the fate of John the Baptist and Jesus is essentially the same in the Gospel of Mark. Mark speaks of John as "preaching," (1:7), but then he is "delivered up" (*paradidonai*) to his enemies (1:14). Thereupon Jesus makes his own debut, like John, "preaching" (1:14). What is his fate? He too must be "delivered up" (*paradidonai*, 9:31; 10:33). As Mark approaches the Passion Narrative, he creates successive scenes in which Jesus predicts his own betrayal and death in Jerusalem. But the disciples cannot understand or accept what he is saying. Peter rebukes him (8:32); the disciples cannot understand his meaning (9:32); James and John can only speak of the glory that is to come (10:37). Finally Jesus asks them: "Are you able to drink the cup that I drink, or to be baptized with the baptism with which I am baptized?" (10:38), clear references to martyrdom. They reply, "We are able" (10:39). Are they?

Now, with the stage set, Mark heads into the Passion Narrative. Jesus provokes the authorities (11:15-17), who begin to conspire against him (11:18). What Jesus has predicted is beginning to take place. Mark enhances the developing tension. Jesus defends his authority against those who would question him (11:27-33). He prophesies against Jerusalem in parables (12:1-12). He gives a provocative answer to the question of whether to pay the tribute (12:13-17). He denounces the scribes (12:38-40). Something bad is going to happen to this man—one can sense it. But he wades deeper into the trouble, true to his cause, unflinching in the face of the growing danger.

Now Mark comes to what is arguably the high point of his entire narrative, at least for his audience: the apocalypse. Here Jesus foretells what is to happen in the future—about a generation away (13:30). When? "When you see the desolating sacrilege set up where it ought not to be (let the reader understand), then let those who are in Judea flee to the mountains" (13:14). Here Mark, with an inside nod to his audience, refers to the imminent destruction of the Jerusalem Temple. He is speaking of the very war that is just now raging around them. When will all of this take place? Now! says Mark. It is happening now! What will it mean for those who are reading these words? Jesus speaks to them out of the past, foretelling the future—their unfolding present:

But take heed to yourselves; for they will deliver you up (*paradi-donai*) to councils; and you will be beaten in synagogues; and you will stand before governors and kings for my sake, to bear testimony before them. And the gospel must first be preached to all nations. And when they bring you to trial and deliver you up (*paradidonai*), do not be anxious beforehand what you are to say; but say whatever is given you in that hour, for it is not you who speak but the Holy Spirit. And brother will deliver up brother to death, and father his child, and children will rise against their parents and have them put to death; and you will be hated by all for my name's sake. But he who endures to the end will be saved. (13:9-13)

It is clear: John preached, and was delivered up; Jesus preached, and was delivered up. Now Mark's readers see their own fate. They will be called upon to preach, and they too will be delivered up.[22] How will they face this fearful prospect? Mark hopes that the martyr's story will now do what it is designed to do. Jesus, the persecuted righteous one, is to be their model. The disciples will flee (14:50). But Jesus will remain faithful to the end. Mark insists that his readers must emulate the steadfast faithfulness of Jesus, true to their cause to the very end. For those who can do this, there is reward: "But anyone who endures to the end will be saved" (13:13b).

This final admonition recalls to mind the words of Epictetus on the death of Socrates: "he is saved by death, not by flight." Mark hopes to convince his readers not to flee. Death may lie before them, but it is not to be feared. This idea, that death must not be feared, is central to the Noble Death tradition. Seneca argued that this was precisely why Socrates chose to face death, even when the opportunity of escape presented itself. In his letter to Lucilius (*On Despising Death*) he writes: "Socrates in prison discoursed, and declined to flee when certain persons gave him the opportunity; he remained there, in order to free humankind from the fear of two most grievous things, death and imprisonment" (*Ep.* 24.4 [LCL]).

This theme is indeed relevant to Mark and his audience. They live in fearful times. Throughout Mark's Gospel fear confronts those who would believe in Jesus. Fear is the enemy, the polar opposite of faith for Mark. "Do not fear, only have faith," says Jesus to those who fear that the ruler's daughter, whom he might have healed, is already dead (5:36). "Why are you afraid? Have you no faith?" asks Jesus when the disciples respond in fear to Jesus' powerful act of calming the sea (4:40).

As Mark's story unfolds, the disciples' fear intensifies. It comes to a head in Mark's depiction of Jesus' last meal with his followers (14:12-26), a scene surely reminiscent of the Socratic tradition. During the meal, Jesus invites his closest friends to eat with him from a common loaf and to drink from a common cup. Mark includes here the words of a Christian ritual that date back at least to the apostle Paul, which identify the broken bread with Jesus' body, and the wine of the cup with Jesus' blood.[23] Mark augments the tradition with words that might have been vaguely familiar from Isaiah's Servant Songs: the wine is Jesus' blood "poured out for many" (14:24).[24] The impending fate of God's Suffering Servant is underscored. They drink from the common cup and form a covenant, a pact sealed in the blood of Jesus. They are ready now to follow him, even into death. But even as they share in these symbols of ultimate commitment, the scene is charged with themes of betrayal and fear. Judas has already plotted to deliver him up (14:10-11; note *paradidonai*), and Jesus knows this and brings it into the midst of their ritual (14:17-21), filling the disciples with doubts and suspicions. As the meal ends, Jesus seems to suggest that this little covenant making has all been a sham. It has meant nothing. They will fail to follow through, he predicts: "You will all fall away" (14:27).[25]

And they do. In the Garden of Gethsemane, when Judas comes to turn Jesus over to the authorities, the other disciples are terrified and flee (14:50). Only Peter remains in the narrative, but just long enough to demonstrate what it really means to collapse in fear. He has promised Jesus, even "if I must die with you, I will not deny you" (14:31). But Jesus' prophecy that Peter will deny him, not once but three times before a rooster crows twice (14:30), now comes to pass as Peter loses his nerve under cross-examination by a slave woman and an anonymous bystander as he lurks outside the high priest's residence where Jesus is being interrogated inside (14:66-72). So much for brave promises made in private rooms. Meanwhile, Jesus alone endures the fate of the suffering righteous one: falsely accused, convicted, and finally beaten and spat upon (14:53-65; cf. Isa 50:4-9).

Fear even stalks the women, who, in contrast to the men who have followed Jesus, have not all fled. They remain, and after the Sabbath has passed they go to the tomb to tend to the body of Jesus (16:1-8). But when they find the tomb empty, they are not emboldened by their discovery. The angel standing guard instructs them to go and tell the disciples what they have seen. But they do not, for they cannot. "They said nothing to anyone, for they were afraid"—*ephobounto gar* (16:8). With this awkward phrase, Mark brings his story to a close with a colossal loose end. It demands the question: Who will have the courage to tell the story? Who will bear witness? Who would be a martyr?

The Glory of Death

In many ways these concerns about survival, fear, and faithfulness were John's concerns as well. The fourth evangelist wrote some years after Mark, but he too faced times that posed a threat to him and his church. It was a time when Jews and Christians were going their separate ways. Jews who were followers of Jesus found themselves having to choose between the security of the larger community in which they lived and the risky human experiment that was the emerging church. John even avers that those who would dare to expose themselves in his community by declaring their belief that Jesus is the Messiah might face death (16:2). The pressure felt by those within John's church was intense. Indeed, some might even have begun to renounce their faith (16:1; 9:22).[26]

Like Mark, John turns to the martyrological tradition to try to shore up the flagging zeal of his folk.[27] In presenting the death of

Jesus as that of a martyr, John had before him many of the same basic elements used by Mark. He probably had a passion narrative similar to that of Mark, likewise built on the idea of God's suffering righteous one. He was a Jew, quite likely from Antioch, and so must have known the Maccabean martyrological tradition well. He was also part of the larger Hellenistic world, with its philosophical discussions of how to die nobly, true to one's cause.

But John's creative act of building his own story of Jesus did not imitate that of Mark. There may be many reasons for this; John is a complex book. One reason, however, is clear. John had a different way of thinking about Jesus; he had a different Christology. In Mark, Jesus is a human being, the Son of man, who is designated as God's Son at the event of his baptism by John the Baptist (Mark 1:9-11). In John, Jesus is not a human being. He is "the Son of God, or God, striding across the earth."[28] He is the Logos of God, God's own Word, at one with God from the beginning of time. Apart from him, nothing in all creation came into being (John 1:1-5). This very "high" Christology may, in part, explain how Jesus faces the final days of his life in John. Through the final chapters of the Gospel, from Gethsemane to the arrest and trial scenes, and finally to the cross, Jesus is in control. In Gethsemane, for example, Judas brings an entire cohort (*speiran*) of Roman soldiers (about 600 men) to arrest Jesus (18:3). But with a word from God's Son—*egō eimi* ("it is I")—they all fall to the ground, powerless before him (18:6). These words, *egō eimi*, are not innocent in John. They are the epiphanic words of self-revelation spoken by the one who is God incarnate. In John, Jesus is no ordinary victim of Roman justice. He is a powerful, willing captive, orchestrating his own death according to a grand plan.

Initially this may seem to diminish the power of Jesus' death as a witness to others. What he, the Logos of God, could do was superhuman, not to be attempted by mere mortals. John does risk this conclusion. But the willingness of a martyr to embrace death, even to orchestrate its arrival, is not without precedent. Socrates rejected his friends' plot to spirit him away from Athens. He chose instead to die nobly, willingly, in control to the end. In the Christian tradition itself, to choose to die, to dream about it, to plan it out, became the highest expression of martyrological zeal. In one famous scene from a third-century Christian martyrological text,[29] the young and beautiful Perpetua, a girl barely past her teens, faces her executioners with a resolve that is almost superhuman. Her executioner is a young gladiator whose hand is trembling so much that he cannot make his sword perform the final deed. So Perpetua, to the astonishment of the crowd, reaches out, takes his hand, and guides the blade to her own throat.[30] Such is the martyr's zeal.

For a community that feels itself under siege, it was no doubt important to think of Jesus as in complete control of the situation. Nonetheless, in presenting Jesus as he does, John risks creating too great a chasm between Jesus, the cosmic Logos of God, and the normal people who must find in their own very human lives the wherewithal to follow Jesus. Thus, even though John's Jesus is in control in this narrative, almost orchestrating the unfolding drama of his death, John still tries to connect the fate of Jesus with that of his audience using martyrological motifs and ideas. Let us take, for example, the way John handles the final days of Jesus in Jerusalem, the ground covered by the Passion Narrative. Jesus and the disciples arrive in Jerusalem in triumphal procession. This much comes from the Passion Narrative. But as he arrives, he is already under a cloud. There is no need of an incident in the Temple to provoke the authorities; Jesus has been provoking them all along with his outrageous words. The threat of death already stalks him (see, e.g., 5:18; 7:19, 25, 32, 44; 8:59; 10:31; 11:45-53). Thus John has moved what would have been the next scene in the Passion Narrative, the Temple incident, up to the opening scenes of the Gospel, using it already in chapter 2 as a kind of first provocative act (2:13-22). Jesus has been arguing, provoking trouble, all along. In the end, even his miracles somehow provoke the authorities who begin to plot his death. Ironically, it is Caiaphas who provides the first hint that Jesus' impending death will not be an ordinary execution. With words invoking the Hellenistic Noble Death tradition of dying for others, the high priest describes Jesus' death as the vicarious death of a martyr:[31] "you do not understand that it is expedient for you that one man should die for the people, and that the whole nation should not perish" (11:50).

With the tension building, Jesus turns to face what awaits him in this last visit to Jerusalem, invoking familiar ideas from the martyrological tradition:

> The hour has come for the Son of man to be glorified. Truly, truly, I say to you, unless a grain of wheat falls to the earth and dies, it remains alone; but if it dies, it bears much fruit. He who loves his life loses it, and he who hates his life in this world will keep it for eternal life. If anyone serves me, he must follow me; and where I am, there shall my servant be also; if any one serves me, the Father will honor him. (12:23-27)

John has packed much into these verses: that in death a life is transformed; that to gain authentic life, one must be willing to part with life, "to hate life in this world"; that anyone who would serve Jesus must follow him, even into death. All of these ideas are developed from the martyrological tradition, as we have seen. Embracing this entire thought is the idea that Jesus' death is not a crisis or a catastrophe to dread. It is to be his moment of glory. Those who follow him into death, God will honor.

This is different from what we have seen in Paul or in Mark, where Jesus' death, though significant in martyrological terms, is still the nadir of the story. It is a crisis to be faced with dignity. In John, Jesus' death is the climax of the story, the moment in which he is to be glorified. And not he alone. In this act God is glorified as well: "Now my soul is troubled. And what should I say—'Father, save me from this hour'? No, it is for this reason that I have come to this hour. Father, glorify your name.' Then a voice came from heaven, 'I have glorified it, and I will glorify it again'" (12:27-28). Here John invokes the memory of Jews throughout time who have been martyred in faithfulness to God: "I have glorified it, and I will glorify it again." To die as a martyr is to glorify God. One sees this in the Maccabean literature (e.g., 4 Macc 1:12; 18:23). To die thus is to bring to oneself honor and glory—this too is a martyrological theme (e.g., 4 Macc 7:9). Glorious is the martyr's death in every respect. This is why John repeatedly refers to Jesus' death as his glorification (e.g., John 7:39; 13:31-32; 17:1).

With such sentiments John wends his way into the Passion Narrative, where we expect to follow, in close succession, the Last Supper, Gethsemane, and finally Jesus' arrest and trial. But before rushing on with the story, John pauses. In John's narrative, Jesus now retreats with his disciples for one final private discourse. The pause is long—chapters 13–17—and includes instruction on how to care for one another, how properly to understand him, and the nature of the world. He gives the disciples one last commandment: "I give you one final commandment, that you love one another. Just as I have loved you, you also should love one another. By this everyone shall know that you are my disciples, if you have love for one another" (13:34-35). And then, again: "This is my commandment, that you love one another as I have loved you. No one has greater love than this, to lay down one's life for one's friends. You are my friends if you do what I command you" (15:12-14).

Here are the basic ideas of the martyrological tradition. The fate of the martyr is united with those who would follow him in life and in death. As Jesus loved, so they are to love. As Jesus died, so must they also be willing to die for one another. His death is a witness to them, an act to be imitated. The relevance of this idea soon becomes clear as Jesus' discourse continues:

> If the world hates you, be aware that it hated me before it hated you. If you belonged to the world, the world would love you as its own. Because you do not belong to the world, but I have chosen you out of the world—therefore the world hates you. Remember the word that I said to you, "Servants are not greater than their master." If they persecuted me, they will persecute you; if they kept my word, they will keep yours also. . . . I have said these things to you to keep you from stumbling. They will put you out

of synagogues. Indeed, the hour is coming when those who kill you will think that by doing so they are offering worship to God. (15:18-20; 16:1-2)

The Farewell Discourse of Jesus in John is a long exposition of John's typical theology: the Logos of God is returning to the place whence he has come. But by lacing these chapters with ideas clearly drawn from the martyrological tradition, John manages to keep Jesus from drifting off into transcendental irrelevance. The Logos is also Jesus, the teacher and martyr. His life and death stand as a witness for how to live and die. As Jesus retires with his disciples and instructs them thus, one cannot help but think of that last meeting of Socrates with his companions. As Jesus goes forth from the upper room to face arrest with dignity, to defy his tormentors with words that witness to his resolve, to defy Pilate himself, one cannot help but think of the heroic witness of Eleazar, denouncing the tyrant whose instruments of torture have become powerless over him. In the end, Jesus dies with dignity. In the final death scene (19:25b-30) there is no cry of anguish, as in Mark. From the cross Jesus calmly sees to his mother's future; he drinks from a bowl of sour wine (again, vague allusions to Socrates' final acts); and then utters the final word: *tetelestai* ("it is finished"). This noble end is not a disgrace. It is a moment of accomplishment, of glory.

To Live and Die with Jesus

For the early followers of Jesus, his death was not simply the death of a victim. Jesus died as a martyr. A martyr (*martys*) is a "witness." For the early followers of Jesus, his death was a witness in a double sense. On the one hand, Jesus' faithfulness to his cause testified to the proposition that there are things worth dying for. Jesus died for God's new empire, that new way of being in the world he tried to exemplify in his words and deeds. His death was an invitation—a dare, really—to others to try to live as he had lived. On the other hand, it testified to the fact that it is possible to face such a death nobly, without fear. The martyr's death is ultimately an act of freedom: freedom from fear. Once one has learned to face death without fear, then there really is nothing to be feared. As Seneca tells his friend Lucilius, "death is so little to be feared, that through its good offices nothing is to be feared."[32] Jesus' death, as a martyr's death, is one that frees one from fear—not only the fear of death, but all such fears that would dissuade one from embracing Jesus' unusual way of thinking about human life and relationships. In this sense, the power of death, and of those who wield its instruments, is vanquished.

For Christians who embraced Jesus' dissident stance over against the empire and its ways, grasping this sense of freedom was very important. If Jesus could face false charges, arrest, torture, and death, even death on a cross, without fear, then what power should these things have over his followers as they pursued that same vision of God's empire for which Jesus had willingly died? As Paul wrote to those followers of Jesus living in the heart of Rome itself:

> If God is for us, then who is against us? He who did not spare his own Son, but gave him up for us all, will he not also give us all things with him? Who shall bring any charge against God's elect? It is God who justifies. Who is to condemn? It is Jesus Christ who died, yes, who was raised from the dead, who is at the right hand of God, who intercedes for us. Who shall separate us from the love of Christ? Shall tribulation, or distress, or persecution, or famine, or nakedness, or peril, or sword? As it is written, "For thy sake we are being killed all day long; we are regarded as sheep to be slaughtered." No, in all these things we are more than conquerors through him who loved us. For I am sure that neither death, nor life, nor angels, nor principalities, nor things present, nor things to come, nor powers, nor height, nor depth, nor anything else in creation, will be able to separate us from the love of God in Christ Jesus our Lord. (Rom 8:31-39)[33]

This is the power of the martyr's death: it enables one to live faithfully to God, free from fear of the consequences that might come from such an act of defiance. The martyr's death is an act that conquers the power of death itself, by showing that death is not to be feared. When one embraces the possibility of the martyr's death, then the martyr's life becomes possible too. This, finally, is the point of seeing Jesus as a martyr. The martyr frees one to live the martyr's life by showing one how to die the martyr's death, free from the all-consuming fear of death. The martyrological tradition gave early Christians a way of using the death of Jesus, terrifying though it was, as a source of power for those who would take up his dissident way of life, and his cause of a new empire of God.

What of those of us who would look to the ancient roots of Christianity for ways to understand Jesus and his fate as somehow significant for our own quest for meaningful existence: could the martyrological tradition prove meaningful even today? Are there things worth dying for? Are there causes worth living for? Certainly these are the questions raised by the ancient tradition of martyrdom. But early Christians did not pose these questions in the abstract like this. They had in mind a particular cause, a particular vision of human existence lived before God that they had come to see in Jesus' words and deeds. They—some—would willingly die for that vision, the empire of God. But the martyrological tradition has also been used to coax people to die for things far less noble, far less worthy than this unusual vision of life. From antiquity to modernity one sees this again and again in Christian history. There is a fine line between the martyr and canon fodder. Is the soldier drafted to fight a war in which he or she does not believe a martyr? Is a suicide bomber who blows up a bus full of anonymous bystanders a martyr?

So what shall we do with the martyrological tradition? Has history rendered us hopelessly cynical about the idea of dying for a cause? Perhaps. Nonetheless, the martyrological tradition remains important. For it offers an understanding of Jesus' death as "vicarious," as "for us," that is quite different from classical theories of atonement. In the martyrological tradition Jesus' death remains utterly connected to his life: he died obedient to his cause. To be moved by such a death is to be moved by the life that led to it. To be saved by such a death is to be set free from the fear that might prevent one from embracing that life as one's own. The life and death of a martyr are meaningless if those who witness them remain unmoved. They become vicarious "for us" only insofar as we embrace them as the life we would dare to lead and the death we would be willing to risk.

We may never be called upon to die for those things in which we believe most deeply. But the martyr's death is only the final act in his or her life. The courage to die for one's convictions is preceded by the courage to live out one's convictions. Martyrdom is not, finally, about death. It is about living life meaningfully, fully devoted to the things one believes in most deeply, free from the various fears, both profound and petty, that would usually dissuade one from such a course. To speak of Jesus as a martyr is to consider the values, ideas, and principles he lived and died for, and the God who comes to life in them, and to ask what it would take to bring that God to life once again in lives we might lead. What would it cost to do this? Would it be worth it? Would it be worth everything?

Sacrifice

Without constant sacrifice, the world would fall apart.
—Stanley K. Stowers,
"Greeks Who Sacrifice and Those Who Do Not"

*Those who will not or cannot conform to the rituals of a society
have no chance in it.*
—Walter Burkert, *Homo Necans*

It is common for Christians today to speak of Jesus' death as a sacrifice. But what do we mean when we speak in this way? Sacrifice is not a ready metaphor in our cultural parlance. How often, for example, does one actually witness the sacrifice of an animal in modern America? The very idea is repulsive to most. I suspect that the act of sacrificing an animal is even illegal in most states. This almost complete absence of sacrifice in our culture poses a difficulty for the theological use of this idea: we have no common cultural understanding of what sacrifice means. Small wonder that when one asks what it means to speak of Jesus' death as a sacrifice, all sorts of ad hoc answers come pouring out, many of which are woven around the modern post-Freudian experience of guilt and the personal quest for a guilt-free existence. Christ's sacrifice becomes the carte blanche by which one might stroll carefree through a world of injustice that demands a word of protest from our muted lips, peremptorily silenced by an insipid persuasion that "our debt has been paid." This is credit-card theology, where Daddy always pays the bill.

If our world is a world devoid of sacrifice, the ancient world of Christian origins was one in which sacrifice was ubiquitous. While strolling through the center of ancient Corinth, for example, as the apostle Paul would have done on any day of the week, one might observe the startling spectacle of animals falling under the sacrificer's ax in any of its temples, great and small. The air would have been pierced by the ritual scream of the women positioned around each high altar, cued to their climactic song by the raised hand of the priest poised to strike the decisive blow. The pleasant smell of roasting viscera and boiling meat would have filled the air, piquing the appetite for that rare taste of meat expertly cooked. Sacrifice was at the center of every ancient Greek city. It was the central theme of Hellenistic public life. It continued to be so throughout the Roman imperial period. The raw experience of sacrifice was constant in antiquity. What would it have meant to speak of Jesus' death as a sacrifice in *that* cultural setting?

Sacrifice in Antiquity

What do we know about the meaning of sacrifice in the ancient world? Surprisingly little, it turns out. Like so many things that form the common stock of a culture, the meaning of sacrifice seems to have been so self-evident that few ever had occasion to expound on it.[1] A good start can be made, perhaps, with mythology. How is it that Greeks came to sacrifice to the gods? The foundational myth occurs in Hesiod's *Theogony*.[2] Here we learn of how Prometheus kills an ox to be shared by gods and mortals, but by trickery and cunning secures for mortals the edible parts of the animal—the meat and the viscera—leaving for the gods only the bones. For this he would suffer a suffering of mythic proportions, chained to his Promethean rock. Those who told the tale, though, appreciated his deed. It is the story, after all, of how mortals, not quite gods, and yet more privileged than the animals, came to eat meat. The significance of sacrifice is, first of all, culinary.[3]

Lest this seem a little disappointing, consider the significance of eating meat in a peasant society. Meat in such a setting is a rare thing. Who gets to eat the meat? Who receives the best parts? How is it distributed? For the Greeks, and for all who were taken up into the sacrificial culture of the Hellenistic world, all of this is wrapped up in their sacrificial practices. Sacrifice was about the eating of meat. Virtually all red meat consumed in a Hellenistic city was sacrificial meat.[4] "To sacrifice" in Greek is also "to feast." "To butcher" in Greek is also "to sacrifice."[5] The *mageiros,* who strikes the blow at the altar, is at once "butcher," "cook," and "sacrificer."[6] This linguistic convergence underscores that for Greeks a sacrifice is a culinary event, and the eating of meat a sacred occasion. How important is sacrifice? How important is food? In a peasant economy, in which ninety percent of people live at subsistence level, food is the all-consuming issue. Who gets it? How much? When? These are the issues negotiated through Hellenistic sacrificial practice.

Consider a typical public festival in a Hellenistic city. Sacrifices would have been organized and financed by the elite of the city, the "first citizens"; the presiding priests come from among their ranks as well. The festival begins with a procession of priest, victim, and participants, with much music, pomp, and celebration. The animal victim is coaxed along, not led; it should come along willingly, implicitly giving its assent to the killing that is to take place. It agrees to the deed again upon arriving at the temple, as the participants shower the animal with handfuls of grain. As it shakes its coat free of the tiny granules that cling to it, this too is taken as a nod of assent. A prayer is offered, then a few hairs are clipped from the animal and cast into the waiting fire—an offering of firstfruits, the *aparchē,* or "beginning," of the sacrifice. Finally, the animal agrees once more before the altar itself, by lowering its head to drink from the water bowl placed before it: the willing victim appears to submit to the blow. This is not a violent act to be resisted. It belongs to the order of things; it is necessary. As the ax is raised, so are the voices of those who surround the proceedings, the women trilling in that distinctive high-pitched way that Westerners today still find both eerie and exciting. The ax falls, doing its work swiftly and cleanly (botching it now would be a very bad omen). The animal falls. Its blood—the animal's life—spills out, but is quickly collected to be sprinkled or poured upon the altar: a life taken is quickly returned to the gods. Now the viscera are efficiently removed. The liver is examined for omens. Then all these delicacies—liver, heart, lungs, spleen, and kidneys—are roasted and immediately consumed by the inner circle of celebrants. The rest of the animal is then butchered and cooked—usually boiled for tenderness. The bones are saved to reconstruct the skeleton, which, wrapped in fat, will be consumed by the altar fires, offering back to the gods their meager share.[7]

Finally, the cooked meat is distributed and the feasting begins. While modern anthropology has tended to focus on the act of killing as the central moment of the sacrifice,[8] for ancients living in a subsistence economy, where food is always an issue, and meat especially is a rarity, this distribution would have been the moment for which everyone was really waiting. In ancient Greece this distribution is said to have proceeded along egalitarian lines, each citizen participant receiving an equal share of the meat.[9] But in later Roman times, when the hierarchical systems of patronage and power, especially in the form of the imperial cult, had reshaped the contours of Hellenistic political life, the distribution would have reflected the top-down brokerage common to that era.[10] The first citizens of the city received the largest, choicest portions, second-rank officials the more common cuts. Further down the social food chain the shares would have become smaller and mean. Outside the circle altogether stood women, noncitizens, children, and foreigners. Their portions would come through those who might connect them to the civic, political, and religious life of the community: their husbands, fathers, and patrons. A sacrifice, finally, expresses and reinscribes the ordering of a community through the most elemental of human necessities: food. Here, as in all times and places, you are what you eat.

Thus the sacrifice, an offering aimed ostensibly at the gods, is also full of effects for the community that surrounds the altar. First of all, it defines the boundaries of the community. Sacrificing together, more than any other tangible act in antiquity, indicates one's membership in a group, whether that be a family, a club, a city, or, finally, an empire. Second, it provides a social index, or map, for the community gathered. Gender distinctions are reinscribed insofar as the inner circle of participants are all male; the very presence of women at the altar would pollute it.[11] And the more elaborate web of social standing, position, and hierarchy is traced out as the food is distributed in proper rank and order. By the end of the day, everyone knows how it is in the world, and all, by their participation, give their assent to this ritually created and ordered world. In the Hellenistic age, it was through sacrifice that culture found its coherence. "This essential act in Greek life is a moment when the world is set in place under the eyes of the gods."[12]

Though the details of sacrificial practice varied from culture to culture, even from city to city, this basic picture held true for most of the peoples of the Mediterranean basin throughout the period of Christian origins. This much was shared across many cultural lines: a sacred priesthood, the killing of a prized animal, the offering of cereal and wine as well, and the distribution of the food. These were the basic elements in Greek and Roman sacrificial practice. Jewish practice differed only in that the foundational sacrifice that created and sustained Israel as a people, by tradition offered originally on Sinai (Exod 24:1-11), and now daily in the Temple (Exod 29:38-46), was a whole burnt offering (*'olah*), consumed entirely by the altar fires as a fragrant gift to satisfy Yahweh. No Promethean trickery here to save the best parts for the human ones; everything "goes up in smoke," to God. But this was just one kind of sacrifice among the Jews. More common, and similar to Mediterranean practice generally, were the frequent "peace offerings" (*zebach shelamim*) to be made from the slaughter of any domesticated animal (Lev 17:1-9). Leviticus makes every slaughter a sacrifice, thus approaching the situation in the Hellenistic cities, where virtually all consumable meat was consecrated. Here too we find the same convergence of vocabulary around the practice of sacrifice and food preparation as one finds in Greek. *Zabach* means both "to sacrifice" and "to slaughter," and the *mizbeach* is both "altar" and "place of slaughter." By this regulation the consumption of meat was mediated through the priests and the Temple. To reiterate, in a peasant culture of subsistence, this is no small thing.

In another class of sacrifices the role of the priesthood in expressing and regulating the boundaries of community life was even more marked. These were the offerings designed to purge the community of the polluting effects of transgression or irregularity. In Israel these included the sin offering (*chatta't*) and the reparation offering (*'asham*). The sin offering was the remedy for conscious violations of the covenant (Lev 4:1—5:13), the reparation offering for unconscious or inadvertent violations (5:14—6:7). In each case the animal was given over to the priests, sometimes to be burned, sometimes to be consumed by the priests themselves (6:17-23). In any event, violation of the established order of things meant for the peasant the sacrifice of something very dear: food.

A similar practice existed among the Romans. Romans were particularly troubled by unusual events—so-called prodigies—that violated their sense of the expected, the normal.[13] A statue is seen to sweat. A goat grows wool. A wild animal runs unexpected through the city. Ravens whine, "as though being strangled."[14] When such things happened, they were to be reported to the Senate, which then decided whether the calamity constituted a true sign of discontent from the gods. If the Senate so decided, the matter was referred to diviners to determine the proper sacrificial remedy, which was then carried out by the priests (all of senatorial rank). Prodigies were usually associated with political, military, or economic crises, and taken to indicate the source of the crisis: divine displeasure. Defining the problem, specifying the remedy, and ultimately wielding the power to restore order and normalcy were prerogatives that lay firmly in the hands of Rome's ruling elite, the Senate.

What if the calamity was so great that no ordinary sacrifice would suffice to restore the divinely ordered world, placate the gods, and save the people from assured destruction? Sometimes nothing less than a *human* sacrifice would do. Many places in ancient Greece had the practice of selecting a person—usually from among the destitute and socially marginal—who might be ritually invested with the sins and transgressions of the people and ceremoniously driven from the city, thus bearing away all that had offended the gods. Such a one was called the *pharmakos*, a term closely related to the neuter noun *pharmakon*, which means drug or healing agent, even "charm." The *pharmakos* was the remedy, the means by which that which ails the city could be dispatched.[15] The Jews, of course, had a similar custom, only performed with a goat rather than an outcast (Lev 16:20-22). In Roman times the execution of a criminal might carry such sacrificial overtones.[16]

More ennobling was a person's *voluntary* sacrifice on behalf of his or her people. We have already learned in the last chapter of the ancient tradition of the Noble Death and martyrdom, and how this played a key role in the interpretation of Jesus' death among his followers. But now we should add that the ancient tradition of dying nobly for a cause, or more commonly for one's city or people, often took on the character of atoning sacrifice as well.[17] This popular theme in Hellenistic literature favors virgins and generals especially. Virgin daughters seem to be offered in pairs; for example, the legendary daughters of Erechtheus, sacrificed to satisfy the anger of Poseidon,[18] or the daughters of Antipoios of Thebes, Androcleia and Alcis, who were said to have sacrificed themselves to save their city.[19] Of generals there are plenty, including the Decii, father, son, and grandson, all of whom, by legend, gave themselves in battle as an expiatory offering (*devotio*) to the gods to save the Roman people.[20] P. Decius (son) summarizes the family legacy in words provided by the Roman historian Livy: "This is the privilege granted to our house that we should be an expiatory sacrifice to avert dangers from the State." This he says as he throws himself into battle against the Gauls. "Now will I offer the legions of the enemy together with myself as a sacrifice to Tellus and the Dii Manes."[21] With that, he says a prayer and spurs

his horse into the heart of the battle and is slain. This was how parti-
sans viewed Cato's death as well, as may be seen in the stirring oration
conjured up by Lucan in his epic poem on the Roman Civil War: "Let
my blood redeem the nations, and my death pay the whole penalty
incurred by the corruption of Rome," says Cato. "My blood, mine
only, will bring peace to the people of Italy and end their sufferings."[22]
His model for such self-sacrifice is Decius: "As hordes of foemen bore
down Decius when he had offered his life, so may both armies pierce
this body, may the savages of the Rhine aim their weapons at me."[23]

As we have seen in the last chapter, Jews had their own martyrs,
whose deaths they came to see as sacrificial in just this way. In the traditions of early Judaism, the great heroes of the Maccabean literature—
the old priest Eleazar, the seven brothers and their mother, all of whom
were tortured to death by Antiochus IV Epiphanes during the early
days of the Maccabean revolt—provide the best-known instance of this
development. It occurs already in one of the earlier Maccabean books,
Second Maccabees (second century B.C.E.). Here the last to die of the
seven brothers confesses, "we [Hebrews] are suffering for our own sins"
(7:32). By their deaths, the seven brothers and their mother hope to
obtain for Israel the mercy of God, and "to bring to an end the wrath
of the Almighty that has justly fallen on our whole nation" (7:37-38).
The idea that these heroes died an expiatory death persisted and
became relevant again during the Roman imperial period. Then
among the Jews of Antioch, the Maccabean martyrs were remembered
once more. In Fourth Maccabees, written during the first century C.E.,
their deaths are regarded as a sacrifice, an expiation for the sins of the
people. Thus the old priest Eleazar prays shortly before he expires, "Be
merciful to your people and let our punishment be a satisfaction on
their behalf. Make my blood their purification and take my life as a
ransom for theirs" (4 Macc 6:28-29).[24] Of his death, and that of the
brothers and their mother, the narrator of this text concludes:
"Through the blood of these righteous ones and through the propitia-
tion (hilastērion) of their death the divine providence rescued Israel,
which had been shamefully treated" (4 Macc 17:22).

These deaths, of course, are examples of the ultimate sacrifice one might make. But in purpose, and sometimes even in form, they are of a piece with those offered around the public altars, however large or small. The very existence of these ancient communities, whether we are speaking of Athens, Rome, or Jerusalem, depends on sacrifice. In Mediterranean antiquity, a community is a group gathered around an altar. The gods have ordered the world and created every people, each in its place. At the center of each place is an altar, the table at which both gods and mortals gather, where food is both offered and consumed. To sacrifice reconfirms this order—a people in their place, together with their gods. But the place must be fit for the gods; it must be holy. This too is part of the ordering work accomplished by sacrifice. In Judaism, the blood of the sacrificial victim had a sanctifying power. Sprinkled on the altar, it had the power to cleanse the place of sin's soiling effect.[25] It removed the dirt—"matter out of place," to quote Mary Douglas.[26] Sacrifice sets things aright; it puts everything and everyone in their proper place. Sacrifice settles things. When the community begins to dissolve and fall apart, there can be only one solution: sacrifice. This is why Cato throws his life down on behalf of the ideals of Republican Rome. It is why Augustus would years later prohibit all manner of strange and upstart private religious associations and permit only the ancient and time-honored collegia of Rome to offer *proper* sacrifices.[27] It is why Eleazar bears up under torture, even death, as a witness to the gravity of following Israel's law. These sacrifices all aim to set things aright. When all is right once again, sacrifice keeps it so. The hearth burns; the animals are brought; everyone eats; the gods are satisfied and so are the mortals.

Jesus the Sacrifice

Now given all this, what would it mean for the followers of Jesus to begin speaking of his death as a sacrifice? First and foremost, we should expect that this kind of talk would have been closely connected to the processes of social formation that were unfolding in the first years of the Jesus movement. It is not an image located in the personal dimensions of ancient life, but in the sphere of public and private *group* life. This is where we should try to explore the image in early Christian usage: in the context of forming communities. How might early gatherings of the Jesus movement have begun to speak of Jesus' death as a sacrifice?

Imagine yourself in a city such as Corinth, walking into a gathering of these early Christians—followers of Jesus, really, for we cannot assume that they have a firm group identity just yet. They gather at week's end, like other groups of common purpose, to eat and to talk.[28] First comes the eating, then the talking. The talk is of one not present, the founder, who is dead. They speak of what he said, and did, and what he stood for and valued. And then the talk turns to his death. The story is told of how it happened. Perhaps it is familiar to you—the death of God's righteous one—tricked, betrayed by friends, suffering a tortured death, but faithful to the end, and finally exalted by God for his faithful witness. We know this as the martyr's story in Jewish tradition, even a noble death among the Greeks. Now it is told of Jesus, too. But what does it mean, really? The talk continues on into the evening. Perhaps someone says something like this:

> For while we were still weak, at the right time Christ died for the ungodly. Indeed, rarely will anyone die for a righteous person—though perhaps for a good person someone might actually dare to die. But God proves his love for us in that while we still were sinners Christ died for us. Much more surely then, now that we have been justified by his blood, will we be saved through him from the wrath of God. For, if while we were enemies, we were reconciled to God through the death of his Son, much more surely, having been reconciled, we will be saved by his life. (Rom 5:6-10)

These are words, of course, from the apostle Paul. They speak on the one hand of the Messiah's willing death—a martyr's death—but at the same time of the reconciling effect that Jesus' death has for those who follow him, unworthy though they may be. This sort of talk, as we have seen, was right at home in the Hellenistic milieu of Christian origins. The martyr's death is not just a death that bears witness to a cause. It can also be a sacrifice reconciling sinners with their God. This is how Lucan understood Cato's death. It is how Jews in Antioch understood Eleazar's death. It is how the followers of Jesus came to understand his death as well.[29]

When such passages in Paul are read today one might easily overlook the martyrological aspects of the text. "Jesus died for our sins" is understood in purely sacrificial terms. But this cheats the context within which this idea was at home, and from which the idea drew much of its power. The saving aspect of the martyr's death cannot be separated from the exemplary aspects of his life. The career of the martyr is in part vicarious precisely through the example it sets for others.[30] Notice that in this instance Paul speaks of the reconciling power of Jesus' death (v. 10a), but it is by his *life* that his followers are saved (v. 10b).

Though Paul's voice is the first one we hear explicating the meaning of Jesus' death in just this way, he was not alone in this, nor was he the first to do it. Earlier in Romans Paul makes rough-and-ready use of an early Christian (pre-Pauline) tradition that brings together the martyrological tradition and these sacrificial notions in the same way (even though the modern translation tradition makes this a little difficult to see on first glance). I will cite it first in the NRSV:

> But now, apart from the law, the righteousness of God has been disclosed, and is attested by the law and the prophets, the righteousness of God through faith in Jesus Christ for all who believe. For there is no distinction, since all have sinned and fallen short of the glory of God; they are now justified by his grace as a gift, through the redemption that is in Jesus Christ, whom God put forward as a sacrifice of atonement by his blood, effective through faith. He did this to show his righteousness, because in his divine forbearance he had passed over the sins previously committed; it was to prove at the present time that he himself is righteous and that he justifies the one who has faith in Jesus. (Rom 3:21-26)

It would be difficult to think of a passage of greater importance to the Reformed understanding of Christian faith. This is unfortunate, for this is also one of the most difficult passages to understand in English, and, unbelievably, even more mystifying in Greek. It is a place—not untypical for Paul—where the apostle blurts out parts of thoughts and traditional formulas with little attention to syntax or sentence formation. What is more, the words he uses are ambiguous in the most crucial places. The NRSV smooths all this out for the reader of English, but in so doing it must resolve all of Paul's broken thoughts and ambiguities into cogent sentences. Here, as much as anywhere in the New Testament, translation is the first act of interpretation, and the only one that really counts.

By far the most important of these ambiguities occurs in the phrase rendered here "faith in Jesus" (vv. 22 and 26). To a believer used to thinking about "justification by faith," this is quite natural. But believing *in* Jesus is probably not what is meant here. A more apt translation of the phrase would be "faith *of* Jesus."[31] Now, how might one be justified, redeemed, or saved by the faith—or faithfulness—*of* Jesus (v. 26)? And how might one speak of God's righteousness being disclosed through the faith *of* Jesus (v. 22)? Again the martyrological context for speaking of Jesus' sacrificial death proves crucial to understanding just what Paul is trying to say. It is always through the martyr's *faithfulness* that God's righteousness is called forth and God's mercy rekindled. It is the martyr's faithfulness, even unto death, that redeems the people in God's eyes. This is the meaning of the first half of the passage. We might translate it as follows:

> But now the just nature of God has been made clear—apart from the law—even though the law and prophets bear witness to it—through the faithfulness of Jesus the just nature of God (has been made clear) to all who have such faith. For there is no distinction, all have sinned and fallen short of the glory of God—but—they have been judged righteous as a gift, by his grace, through the redemption that is in Jesus Christ. . . . (vv. 21-24)

The thought is not yet crystal clear because Paul is fumbling with the language, trying to use a tradition, but qualifying and explaining it all the way through. But Paul seems to be working with the idea, common in the Hellenistic era, that one person's faithfulness could call forth mercy from the gods. This becomes clearer as Paul continues:

> whom God proposed as a sacrifice, because of his [Jesus'] faithfulness—at the cost of his blood. In passing over former sins—in his divine forbearance—God thus demonstrated his just nature . . . (Rom 3:25)

Here it is not as though God sends his son Jesus to earth with the purpose of being a sacrifice, as might be suggested by the NRSV ("God put forth . . .").[32] Rather, God observes the faithfulness of Jesus and proposes that his blood be treated as an expiatory sacrifice. The martyr becomes a sacrifice. Thus Paul finishes the thought:

> as proof of his [God's] just nature in the present time, showing that he himself is just and declares righteous the person who is so from the faith of Jesus. (Rom 3:26)

This last phrase, "from the faith of Jesus," I have left just as vague as Paul himself leaves it. It could mean that the follower of Jesus is declared righteous because Jesus was faithful unto death, and so atoned for the sins of those who follow him.[33] On the other hand, it could mean that the follower is declared righteous if she or he too demonstrates the same kind of faith as that shown by Jesus.[34] The latter seems to fit Paul's argument better, though it chafes against traditional Reformed theology. Indeed, in the next chapter of Romans Paul will offer Abraham as an example of one who was justified by his (own!) faithfulness. The latter interpretation also seems to fit better into the martyrological framework within which these ideas are offered. The martyr's death is expiatory, and so satisfies God; but it is vicarious also by its exemplary nature: it shows the kind of faithfulness that is pleasing to God, and is thus to be emulated.

Given what we have seen in the Hellenistic world—including early Judaism—it is not at all difficult to imagine how Jesus the martyr became Jesus the sacrifice. And given the ubiquity of sacrifice in ancient life, it is easy also to see how this idea could have flourished in Christian circles and taken on a life of its own. As the people of the Jesus movement began to reflect on this idea of Jesus as a sacrifice, they did not always do so in an explicitly martyrological framework. For example, in Romans 8:3 Paul can speak of God sending his son to be a "sin offering" (*hamartia*), thus detaching sacrifice from its martyrological context and grafting it into the idea of the descending/ascending redeemer sent from God. He speaks similarly in 2 Corinthians 5:21: "For our sake he made the one who knew no sin into a *sin offering*, in order that in him we might become the righteousness of God." Here the cultic context of sacrifice shows its influence. Now Jesus is the perfect sacrifice, unblemished, without sin, as must be all victims offered to satisfy God's anger. All of this would have been easily understood by the Jews, Greeks, Romans, and others who came into contact with Christianity. The metaphor was as common as life itself.

Why Sacrifice?

But this answers the question of *how* early Christians came to speak of Jesus as a sacrifice: it was probably in connection with the understanding of Jesus' death as a martyr. But this leaves many more questions yet unanswered. Why did this sacrificial metaphor prove to be so powerful for Jesus' followers in coming to grips with their own existence in the wake of his violent death?

To explore this question further we will need once again to visit that imaginary early Christian gathering in Corinth, paying close attention to what is said, and by whom. Since sacrifice is about eating, it is not surprising that we find some interesting things said about sacrifice in connection with the meal part of this gathering. As the meal begins we learn that it is a commemorative meal. As the first loaf is broken, someone says: "The Lord Jesus on the night when he was betrayed took a loaf of bread, and when he had given thanks, he broke it and said, 'This is my body that is for you. Do this in remembrance of me'" (1 Cor 11:23-24). A broken body, offered "for you." The martyrological theme, with its sacrificial overtones, is clear.[35]

But then, after the meal someone speaks a word about the last cup of wine as well: "This cup is the new covenant in my blood. Do this, as often as you drink it, in remembrance of me" (1 Cor 11:25). Now the sacrificial overtones take on a more distinctive cast. The sacrifice of Jesus' blood is to be understood in terms of the Jewish covenant sacrifice, the sacrifice offered at Sinai that created the bond between the people of Israel and Yahweh, and in so doing, created Israel as a people (Exodus 24), or perhaps the talk of a "new covenant" is to echo the prophetic renewal tradition (Jeremiah 31). The words explicitly invoke the Jewish tradition, but the idea that sacrifice creates, defines, and delineates a people is not unique to Judaism, as we have seen. This is the basic function of sacrifice in the Hellenistic world. It creates community. To speak of Jesus as a sacrifice is to recognize, first, that it is in him that this new community finds it existence. His death draws them together. But how?

The words we have just read from Paul are repeated almost verbatim in the Gospel of Mark. There they are found in a poignant depiction of the last time Jesus eats with his closest followers gathered for the traditional Passover meal just outside Jerusalem (Mark 14:12-31, especially vv. 22-25). Their narrative setting gives them more power yet: Passover commemorates the birth of Israel, the creation of a new people. Another detail underscores the orchestration: those gathered with Jesus are twelve in number, like the original tribes of Israel. Mark sees this as the moment when a new people is born. But this new people consists not just of "the twelve." This symbolic meal is presaged by two meals in Mark involving great throngs of people of every sort, stuck in the wilderness, hungry, and yet miraculously fed by Jesus

(6:30-44; 8:1-10). He is, for Mark, a new Moses, re-creating the passage from bondage to freedom.[36] All of this is fairly straightforward.

But to catch the full effect of what Mark is doing through these passages one should cast an eye to the sort of people who inhabit Mark's narrative, who are brought with Jesus on the journey and joined with him in the new community. There are many ordinary people—the ever-present "crowd," in Mark's story. But there are others, too, whom Mark names and calls attention to especially: lepers, the demon-possessed, foreigners, women—even menstruating women. This table, this meal, this sacrifice is for the unclean and any who would deign to eat with "unclean hands" (Mark 7:2). As he approaches Jerusalem and his final meal there, Jesus warns that he will have to die for what he has been doing. At one point he takes a child—perhaps a street urchin—embraces it, and says: "Whoever welcomes one such child in my name welcomes me, and whoever welcomes me, welcomes not me, but the one who sent me" (Mark 9:37). The table he would die for is one to which even children are invited. All of this is very important. For when this table is transformed into an altar, it will play host to a sacrifice that is for the unclean, the marginal, and the unimportant.

In my view, this is crucial to understanding just why the followers of Jesus found it meaningful to think of his death as a sacrifice. Like a sacrifice, his death created of his followers a community who would be devoted to the same things to which Jesus devoted himself. In this way Jesus' martyrdom could be thought of as a sacrifice, and their meals to commemorate his death, as sacrificial meals. But there is more: they thought of his death not just as a covenant sacrifice. It was also expiatory—an atoning sacrifice. Such a sacrifice removes the stain of the unclean, the offense of the sinner. Just think of the makeup of one of these early communities gathered in Jesus' name. In addition to lepers, the demon-possessed, foreigners, and women, there were also prostitutes, tax collectors, and sinners. Various unclean types turn up in the narratives of these early communities—tanners, for example. Slaves, too, were part of the mix. Paul says of the Corinthian community, "Consider your call, brothers and sisters: not many of you were wise by human standards, not many were powerful, not many were of noble birth" (1 Cor 1:26). This statement of course indicates that some in the Corinthian community were indeed persons of wealth and power, but Paul stresses that most of those who had come to make up this community were *not*. They were "weak," "despised," "nothings" in the world (1 Cor 1:27-28). Those who were "of noble birth" were choosing quite consciously to take leave of their privileged social location by associating with "the low and despised in the world." Paul himself is perhaps the most obvious example of this. He was probably a person of means, educated, perhaps even a Roman citizen, but by his own choice to join a disreputable religious movement he became, in his own words, "the scum of the earth" (1 Cor 4:13). For these "nothings" and those who chose to associate with them, Jesus' death became the sacrifice that made them something: clean, redeemed, drawn together in a community of adopted children of God (Rom 8:14-17).

Imagine a prostitute in the following of Jesus. She comes into this movement, is welcomed to the table, and becomes part of a new community. She—an unclean prostitute—is, for the first time, considered clean. In the company of Jesus she is human. She is no longer an expendable piece of meat, no longer a prostitute. Then Jesus is killed, crucified as a common criminal. Now she must decide: is what she experienced over now, or was it real—real enough to continue as a reality for her? Is she clean or not? Is she a prostitute or not? The city that knows her is of no help to her. A patron who wants what he thinks he deserves from a prostitute says, "You *are* a prostitute. You think you are not? You think you are clean just because Jesus said you were? That's a joke! He's dead, and you're a prostitute. You always were, and you always will be, scum." Here is her challenge. So she says, "I am not a prostitute. I am not unclean. You want something for my sins? You want a sacrifice to atone for me? *Jesus* is my sacrifice. His death was 'for me.' His blood atones for everything I ever did, and everything you ever did to me. You think he was killed—a common, unclean criminal execution—but I say his death was a sacrifice . . . for me." So she gathers at week's end with others who knew Jesus: lepers, tanners, fishmongers, tax collectors, slaves, unaccompanied women, maybe a few street urchins. They eat a meal like they ate with Jesus, they remember what he died for, and they convince themselves once again that it was all true. His death becomes the sacrifice that makes them clean and whole, worthy to come to the table—now "altar"—and eat in the presence of God.

We Abstain!

Early Christian meals might naturally have been saturated with talk of sacrifice. This was, after all, the central theme of sacred meals in antiquity. But now we must attend to something quite peculiar about these early meals. Indeed, all this talk about sacrifice could easily deflect attention away from what is by far the most striking, and from the ancient point of view, most disturbing aspect of these gatherings: in early Christian worship there is, in reality, no sacrifice. No animals are killed. No libations are poured on an altar. There is no altar. A religion without sacrifice: it is not just unusual in the Hellenistic world, it is subversive.

To understand the significance of this great absence in early Christian worship one must recall all that was said earlier about sacrifice and the central role it played in Hellenistic culture. This was not simply a matter of religious sensibility, of style, or of taste. One must think beyond the stark separation of sacred from secular that so marks the social geography of modern Western life. Such a divide did not exist for ancients. Sacrifice was the central expression of ancient religious life, but through sacrifice the social and political world was also given its definitive shape and organization. The world, in this conception, is divinely ordered and maintained, and the human role in this divinely ordained stasis is to sacrifice. "Without constant sacrifice, the world would fall apart."[37]

Practically speaking, sacrifice functioned thus by creating and managing the reality of *place*. An altar is first of all a place, a center for communal life. To be associated particularly with a place, a center, is to be located in the culture and to have an identity. Of course, one might be located multiply in a culture, with several overlapping identities. One might be a citizen of a polis—thus located in a city. One might also be a Roman citizen, part of the empire. Most people had families, yet another location. In addition there were various other temples and religious associations to which one might belong. Each of these "places" revolved around an altar at which sacrifices were offered on a regular basis, from the family shrine, to the city hearth, to the great imperial temples dedicated to the gods Roma and Augustus. To gather at an altar was to mark one as belonging to a particular place.

This was true in a geographic sense, but also in terms of social location. Not everyone could approach the great altar of Athena in Athens. Within the groups gathered at various levels of social and political importance, a social ordering was reflected in the ceremony and, most importantly, in the distribution of the meat and the partaking of the meal. Through sacrificial practice, the whole world was set in place, and each person located somewhere within it. In the Roman imperial period this was especially crucial. For in a totalitarian, strongly hierarchical regime it is above all imperative to know that everyone has a place, and is in fact *in place*. The maintenance of imperial power and control depends utterly on this. The Roman historians Beard, North, and Price summarize what was at issue in the sacrificial practices of the empire:

> What was at stake for emperors, governors, and members of civic elites was the whole web of social, political, and hierarchical assumptions that bound imperial society together. Sacrifices and other religious rituals were concerned with defining and establishing relationships of power. Not to place oneself within the set of relationships between emperor, gods, elite and people

was effectively to place oneself outside the mainstream of the whole world and the shared Roman understanding of human- ity's place within that world. Maintenance of the social order was seen by the Romans to be dependent on maintenance of this agreed set of symbolic structures, which assigned a role to peo- ple at all levels.[38]

Earliest Christians, by choosing not to sacrifice, refused to place themselves within the "web of social, political, and hierarchical assumptions that bound imperial society together." They did this by omitting sacrifice from their own religious life. They refused thus to "place" themselves. But more significantly, they did this by refusing to participate in the whole public and private structure of sacrificial life. They would not attend sacrifices in the local temples. They would not sacrifice to the emperor or his gods. Most importantly, they would not eat the meat that came from the sacrifice of animals to the gods.[39]

This matter of eating sacrificial meat deserves closer scrutiny, for within early Christian groups it became a matter of great dispute. By understanding what was at stake in eating such meat, we might better understand the significance of Christian abstinence from it.

To begin, we should recall three things. First, in an agrarian peas- ant culture meat is a rare thing. People who live at a subsistence level do not eat much meat; any opportunity for such a rich source of sus- tenance was therefore highly prized and cause for much celebration. Second, the consumption of meat—what portion, how much, how often—was directly related to one's social location. Meat was expen- sive; it is as simple as that. Gerd Theissen makes this point by quoting from the rabbinic tractate *b. Ḥullin* 84a: "A man having one *maneh* may buy a *litra* of vegetables for his bowl; if ten a *litra* of fish; if fifty *maneh* a *litra* of meat."[40] Grain is basic. Vegetables are a step up from that. Fish is a luxury. But meat is in a class all by itself. Finally, given these realities, it is quite understandable that in the Hellenistic world, the consumption of meat was indeed always a special occasion, marked in its significance by sacrifice. In fact, as we have already seen, virtually all the meat consumed in the Hellenistic world would have derived from sacrifice. There were great celebrations involving public sacrifices to commemorate great events; there were regular events on the sacred calendar of the empire or of individual cities; there were games and contests; there were smaller gatherings of religious associations and collegia; there were private, "invitation only" gatherings at the great temples and their accompanying banquet facilities.[41] These were the occasions at which meat was made available; each began with a sacrifice, from which the meat was distributed. If an altar marks one's place, it is the meat of sacrifice that draws one close and holds one in place.

Small wonder that the issue of whether one should eat meat that came from a sacrifice emerged as significant for early Christians. Eating meat—publicly—was to involve oneself in the whole web of social and political life, and the religious substance that held it all together. It was more than the issue of practicing idolatry, seen, as it usually is, as an abstract or purely theoretical religious issue. To eat meat was to participate in the world, the empire, and all that it stood for. This was the empire that had executed Jesus as a common criminal. This was the empire that would not tolerate the vision of a new empire so treasured by his followers. To eat meat was to cross the line, to "re-place" oneself in the world from which one had just taken leave. To eat meat, to participate in sacrifice, was to participate in the great cultural project of sustaining the world *as it is*. How could the followers of Jesus do this if they looked forward to another, very different world to come?

Apparently, some did find a way, for the record shows that this was a matter of dispute in various Christian communities. Theissen's analysis clarifies why.[42] For peasants, and even more so for the marginal and expendable types who became part of these communities, to pass up any opportunity for food would have been a grave choice. If you were hungry already, to turn away from the pleasant smell of roasting meat was almost too much to ask. And if you were among the few people of means who joined these communities, abstaining from meat would have meant severing all ties and relationships binding you securely into the social and political web that had nurtured you and

treated you so well. It would have meant extricating yourself from all
patronal relations, all peer associations, all institutional sources of
support. For such a person, the loss of place would have involved taking leave from a place that had in so many ways been rewarding. Eating
sacrificial meat was more than consumption, more than mere worship.
It meant conviviality, commensality, and community.

We first encounter eating sacrificial meat as an issue in Paul's early
Corinthian correspondence. It is a little surprising that Paul should
have such a strong reaction to the practice of eating meat that had
been offered to an idol. True, Jews typically did not eat meat that had
been offered to a pagan god,[43] but Paul had notoriously dispensed
with Jewish dietary practices that would hinder commensality
between Jew and Greek (Gal 2:11-14). Nonetheless, in this case he is
adamant that members of the Corinthian churches should not eat
sacrificial meat. The situation calls for explanation.

Some in the Corinthian community have apparently justified eating sacrificial meat on the grounds that the gods to whom the sacrifice had been made were not really gods after all, and so their
participation in such activities could not compromise their devotion
to the one true God (1 Cor 8:4-6). Paul is not convinced by this explanation, even though he grants that in theory it might be true. He
knows that this is not finally a theoretical matter. Rather, he is concerned about the consequences such activity will have for the whole
community. He asks, "What if someone who doesn't share your
sophisticated theoretical understanding[44] of these things sees you
eating at a temple feast and thinks, if it is all right for him to do that,
why shouldn't I?" (8:10). Paul is realistic here: he knows that meat is a
powerful draw, powerful enough to draw people away from his
abstaining, countercultural community. So, he concludes, "If food is
a cause of their falling, I will never eat meat" (8:13). Paul clearly knows
what meat eating means in his culture: it is about finding one's place
in the community; it is about participation. To be at table is to be
united with those who share the table. Thus later in his argument he
says of their own meals: "The cup of blessing that we bless, is it not a

sharing in the blood of Christ? The bread that we break is it not a sharing in the body of Christ? Because there is one bread, we who are many are one body, for we all partake of the one bread" (10:16-17).

Eating in this sacral way is about expressing one's place, one's belonging to a community. Those who commune together are partners, he argues, and, even though the pagan gods are not really gods, but demons, "I do not want you to be partners (*koinōnous*) with demons," he says (10:20b). Paul is not concerned here with mystical or physical union with lesser deities (by consuming the flesh of the deity, for example). Rather, he speaks in a manner reflecting Hellenistic sacrificial practice. To participate in a sacrificial meal is to be at table with one's chosen companions (*koinōnoi*), including the god, who is also present at the meal. In such meals it was common to set aside certain portions of the meat, placing them on the god's table, or *trapeza*—hence the common name *trapezōmata* for these portions.[45] "You cannot partake of the table (*trapezēs*) of the Lord and the table (*trapezēs*) of demons," he argues (10:21b). Paul clearly knows, as everyone of his culture did, that eating meat is a public statement of belonging. Notice, as his argument continues to resolution, that Paul is not concerned about eating meat in private, where the question would become a purely theoretical question of principle (10:23-27). His concern, rather, is those *public* occasions when eating meat could be seen as a statement (10:28-29). When it comes to that, one's statement should be clear and unequivocal: we abstain![46]

Paul's measured approach to this question would have sounded wishy-washy and weak-kneed to the early Christian prophet responsible for Revelation. From the letters attached to the beginning of the Apocalypse proper we can see that eating sacrificial meat had also emerged as an issue in the churches of western Asia Minor, to which the letters are addressed. It appears specifically in two of these letters, the letter to Pergamum (2:14) and the letter to Thyatira (2:20). In each case the prophet is adamant. Against such persons who eat sacrificial meat the heavenly Christ will make war "with the sword of my mouth" (2:16). At Thyatira the practice is apparently allowed by a woman prophet, whom John insults with the name "Jezebel" and promises to "strike her children dead" (2:23)—a reference presumably to her followers. These searing words are to be understood within the context of Revelation as a whole, which portrays the prophet as the most ardent defender against a great cultural onslaught that was challenging the integrity of these churches at the end of the first century. This was probably during the reign of Domitian, who insisted on order and cultural uniformity as a way of holding off the chaos that always threatened so large an empire as Rome's. Christians who refused to participate in local cults suffered persecution and martyrdom along with all dissidents of that period.[47] But the prophet John would not brook any cultural accommodation whatsoever, even in these extreme circumstances. By the end of the Apocalypse, one can only conclude that martyrdom is preferable by far to the horrors that await those who cave in and "worship the beast" that is Rome.

We are fortunate to have from about that same time a record of just such a confrontation between Christian dissidents and the empire, but told from the point of view of the empire itself. It rings remarkably true to the picture one gets from Revelation. Pliny the Younger governed the Roman province of Pontus-Bithynia early in the second century C.E. Among his letters to the emperor Trajan we find the first mention of Christians in pagan literature. Christians had come to Pliny's attention because they had formed illegal "political associations." Pliny investigated. He rounded up several members of the group, but discovered only

> that they were in the habit of meeting on a certain fixed day before it was light, when they sang in alternate verses a hymn to Christ, as to a god, and bound themselves by a solemn oath, not to do any wicked deeds, but never to commit any fraud, theft, or adultery, never to falsify their word, nor deny a trust when they should be called upon to deliver it up; after which it was their custom to separate, and then reassemble to partake of food—but food of an ordinary and innocent kind. (*Ep.* 10.96 [LCL])

This picture was confirmed for Pliny when he tried "to extract the real truth" by torturing two of the movement's leaders, both female slaves. Were they harmless, or dangerously seditious? Pliny devised a test: the accused should repeat an invocation to the gods, offer adoration to the image of the emperor and the gods, and finally curse Christ. Many did this; but others did not. The latter Pliny ordered executed. This is the true test of sedition: will they sacrifice to the emperor and the gods or not? Why this? As Pliny notes a little later in the letter, before his intervention the temples of the region had all but been abandoned, their festivals neglected, and sacrificial animals had "met with but few purchasers." This was the problem. The Christian refusal to sacrifice struck right at the very heart of Hellenistic civilization and the Roman imperial system that had been built upon its trusses. The altar, sacrifice, meat: without these the Hellenistic world would have fallen into chaos. If there was one thing that Rome feared, it was chaos.

Thus it was that the Christian refusal to sacrifice would remain a point of conflict with the empire for as long as sacrifice remained at the center of public religious and political life. We encounter it again, not surprisingly, at the center of the first great systematic persecution of Christians during the reign of Decius (249–251 C.E.), under whom many Christian dissidents were martyred. We have from that period a papyrus document attesting to the vindication of a certain (presumably) Christian suspect, which illuminates the issues involved. The document, a certificate of sorts, is dated to 250 C.E., and comes from the Fayum district of Egypt, where Christians were required to appear before a local commissioner and perform the requisite sacrifices to satisfy the imperial edict. The "certificate of sacrifice" reads as follows:

> To those chosen to superintend the sacrifices in the village of Alexander's Island; from Aurelius Diogenes, son of Sabatus, of the village of Alexander's Island, aged seventy-two, with a scar on his right elbow. I have always sacrificed to the gods; and now in your presence in accordance with the terms of the edict I have

sacrificed and [poured a libation] and have [tasted] the sacrificial victims. I request you certify this. Farewell. I, Aurelius Diogenes, have presented this petition.[48]

From this we may thus infer the requirements of the edict: one must sacrifice to the gods, pour a libation of wine, and eat of the sacrificial meat. These were the spiritual essentials necessary to holding the whole imperial system together. It is noteworthy that nothing is said here of worshiping the emperor. Loyalty, per se, was not the nub of the issue. The issue was whether you were part of the ongoing, recognized religious and social life of the empire. Beard, North, and Price comment:

> Decius did not specify which gods were to be the recipients of the sacrifices—and it would seem that local gods were as acceptable as specifically Roman ones. In this case the demand was not that Christians should worship Roman deities, but they should participate in the sacrificial system as a whole with its offering of incense, pouring of libations and tasting of sacrificial meat. Sacrifice (not particular gods or festivals) here delimited and paraded the true subjects of Rome.[49]

Taking Leave

Many Christians in the early years of the church did not consider themselves to be true subjects of Rome. They recalled Jesus' proclamation of another empire, an empire of God, and looked forward to the day when the empire they had come to despise would cease to be. This is the spirit in which one should understand the Christian refusal to sacrifice. Why was this spirit so strong among early Christians?

Jonathan Z. Smith has noticed something about religion in the Hellenistic world that may help us to understand this dissident ethos more clearly. Smith observes that in the world of antiquity there are two kinds of religion: he calls them the "locative" type and the "utopian" type.[50] Central to the locative type is the concept of place—

locale. These ancient, tradition-steeped religions center on a place—a city, an altar, a hearth. But they also give place; they locate people by orienting them to a place, and assigning each a place in the divinely ordered world. Sacrifice was *the* expression of "locative" religion, as we have seen. This is why sacrifice was important to Rome, why Rome recognized local cults and encouraged them, and why Rome cultivated its own sacrificial traditions, disseminated them throughout the empire, and integrated the figure of the emperor into this sacrificial legacy. It was, finally, the emperor who ordered the world, and to him that each owed his or her place in the world that was.

But many in this finely tuned world of empire did not like their place. It was a world that thrived on the backs of slaves. It was a world that had little use for the disabled, for abandoned children too young for labor, for women cast outside the world of men, for the sick, the weak, and the mentally ill. In a world so fixed on "place," it was a time particularly prone to "*dis*-place." War, social upheaval, and economic coercion all disrupted the personal lives of millions of people, leaving them without place, or in a new and strange place that did not feel like home. For such people the locative religions simply—sometimes suddenly—lost their relevance. Why rejoice in place, when the place you occupy is no cause for celebration? For such persons, this new experience of place called for a "radical revaluation of the cosmos."[51] Smith speaks of a "cosmic paranoia" that begins to set in—though one should wonder whether an ancient slave's experience of the world as turned utterly against him could justly be called "paranoia." Among such people there emerged a new way of being religious. Smith calls this the "utopian" way, understood in terms of the original Greek meaning of this word: "no place." This way of being religious centers not on place, but on *leave-taking*. It is diasporic, mobile, transitional. In a more speculative mode it contemplates departure from the world that is; it hopes for a better place. The religions of this type are "savior" religions, for the most part, in which a savior descends to earth from the heavenly realms to lead the lost to a new and better place, their true and final "home."

In the Hellenistic world there were many such religions, or branches of older, locative religions, that responded to the experience of being "no place." Christianity was one. Its memory of its own origins was of a radical leave-taking—from village, home, family—in those who followed Jesus. Many of its early leaders were itinerants, like Paul. Its rank and file included slaves, prostitutes, "sinners," the unclean, the disabled, unattached women, and many others who, by their association with such unseemly, un-placed types, found themselves taking leave of the places they had been taught to honor as their own. Not all or even many of these early Christians literally left their homes and families. But their dissidence took a form that was perhaps far more threatening than the itinerant life of the wandering beggar. They took leave of the altar. For the Roman governor, Pliny, this was the crisis. And who did he find leading this exodus-in-place? Two female slaves. Is there a worse place to be in the ancient world than the place of a female slave? This is one of the most remarkable things about Christianity as it unfolded in the days of the Roman Empire: it inspired people to consider their place in the world and to question it. Even slaves found in this movement the wherewithal to see their place as really "no place," and to hope, imagine, and perhaps even begin to live into a new place. But the first steps in this journey were always the most daring: to step away from the altar and into the chaos of really having "no place."

For the followers of Jesus, his death became a powerful moment of clarity. When Jesus was executed as a dissident in the Roman Empire, what became clear to them was that the world they had known could not tolerate the radical reordering implied in the way Jesus had spoken to them about human life and relationships. The Roman Empire could not tolerate the empire of God. So they took leave. They left the empire and their assigned places in it, and they stopped doing the thing that created, affirmed, and maintained the whole imperial placement system: they stopped sacrificing.

This act became the occasion for much interpretive work. Thus early Christians soon discovered in the Jewish prophetic tradition an antisacrificial message that spoke truth to them. One can see this, for example, in the Gospel of Matthew, where the narrative occasion says much about the social context in which this critique of sacrifice became most relevant. Matthew sets the scene: Jesus is dining with "tax collectors and sinners," giving place to those who have no place at a clean and respectable table. His opponents complain to his disciples: "Why does your teacher eat with tax collectors and sinners" (Matt 9:11)? But Jesus overhears them, and replies for them, "Go and learn what this means, 'I desire mercy, and not sacrifice'" (Matt 9:13, citing Hos 6:6). What does this mean? Of what relevance could sacrifice have to this situation? A meal begins with sacrifice. A sacrifice insures that the meal is respectable, clean, with participants that are all respectable and clean. With the sacrifice, everyone is "placed" at the table. But a "sinner" is without place, unclean—"matter out of place." This may have been true for many in the Jesus movement. For those without proper place, and those who chose to associate with them, sacrifice became an encumbrance, and finally irrelevant.

But the death of Jesus also gave his followers a less obvious and more ironic opening for critiquing the culture of sacrifice. We have seen how early Christians could come to speak quite naturally of Jesus' death as a martyr's death, with atoning significance for his followers. We have also seen how they could contemplate their existence as a new community, and extend the sacrificial metaphor using, from the Jewish world, the concept of covenant sacrifice. Jesus became for them the sacrifice that drew them close to God and to one another. But even while working this out, early Christians were also aware that the death of their Jesus was not really a sacrifice. He died on a cross, not an altar. He died battered, pierced, and torn, not a perfect, unblemished lamb, a virgin, or even a hero. The place of his sacrifice was not the innermost *sactum sanctorum* of the Temple, but a stinking pile of bones and bodies outside the city walls. Consider the irony of claiming that this death was a sacrifice. Indeed, it was an antisacrifice.

In the Epistle to the Hebrews the irony of this claim is played out most fully. Here, in one of the few texts in the New Testament where one finds any sustained reflection on the idea of Jesus as sacrifice, we can see how early Christians could critique the culture of sacrifice and at the same time speak of Jesus' death as a sacrifice of a higher, spiritual order. In this remarkable text the whole breadth of the sacrificial tradition comes into play. Jesus' death is an atoning sacrifice (e.g., 9:11-14); it is a covenant sacrifice (e.g., 9:15-22); and finally, it becomes the sacrifice to end all sacrifices:

> Thus, when he came into the world, he said, "Sacrifices and offerings you have not desired, but a body you have prepared for me [cf. Ps 40:7-9]; in burnt offerings and sin offerings you have taken no pleasure [cf. Lev 4:14] . . . ," then he added, "See, I have come to do your will." He abolishes the first in order to establish the second. And it is by God's will that we have been sanctified through the offering of the body of Jesus Christ once for all. (Heb 10:5-6, 9-10)

For the author of Hebrews, the sacrifice of Christ is the end of sacrifice: "For by a single offering he has perfected for all time those who are sanctified" (10:14). What is left but to draw near to God "in full assurance of faith" (10:22). Ironically, sacrifice is brought to an end by sacrifice itself.

This spiritualization of sacrificial concepts, and its implied withdrawal from sacrificial practice, is often seen today by Christians as central to the idea that Christianity has superseded Judaism and gone beyond it. Yet the authoritative Scriptures to which the author of this epistle appeals, and the techniques he uses to explicate them, are all Jewish.[52] Hebrews, in my view, is not an anti-Jewish tract aimed at "Judaizers."[53] Rather, from *within* the Jewish tradition itself the author of Hebrews encourages an antisacrificial ethos in the midst of a broader Hellenistic culture that depended on sacrifice to create and order its social world. This was appropriate, for whoever the original addressees of this epistle might have been, it is clear that they had at some point run afoul of the current social map and those charged with its maintenance. They have suffered public shaming and ridi-

cule, imprisonment, and dispossession (10:32-34), a common fate
for those who dared to assume a dissident stance over against the
empire, who refused to accept their assigned place. They have also
begun to weaken in their resolve (10:23-25). Under these circumstances, the author of the Epistle to the Hebrews offers parenesis
structured around themes that are fitting to the dissident life: bold-
ness (*parrēsia*),[54] endurance (*hypomonē*),[55] hope (*elpis*),[56] and faithfulness (*pistis*).[57]

In Hebrews 11 an elegant encomium on the virtue of faithfulness
underscores the importance for these early Christian dissidents of
accepting the utopian (no-place) implications of what they had chosen to do. In it, the author delves into the great Jewish epic tradition
of leave-taking and associates it with the challenge of being resolute
and faithful. Of Abel, Enoch, Noah, and Abraham he says:

> These all died in faith, not having received what was promised,
> but having seen it and greeted it from afar, and having acknowl-
> edged that they were strangers and exiles on the earth. For people
> who speak thus make it clear that they are seeking a homeland. If
> they had been thinking of that land from which they had gone
> out, they would have had opportunity to return. But as it is, they
> desire a better country, that is, a heavenly one. Therefore God is
> not ashamed to be called their God, for he has prepared for them
> a city. (11:13-16)

The author continues with Moses, the Israelites, Rahab, and others,
finally turning to matters that may have more direct relevance to the
fate of dissidents living in his own community of faith:

> Some were tortured . . . , mocked, scourged, in chains and impris-
> oned . . . , stoned, sawn in two, killed with the sword, they went
> around in skins of sheep and goats, destitute, afflicted, poorly
> treated—of them the world was not worthy—wandering over
> deserts and mountains, and in dens and caves of the earth. (Heb
> 11:35-38)

In the epic tradition of Israel, faithfulness often means accepting rejection, being displaced, wandering in search of new and promised lands, new places with new altars. Out of this tradition, the author of Hebrews builds an ethos fitting for people who had taken leave of those altars around which they had once found their place. They are now "strangers and exiles," whom Ernst Käsemann so aptly named in his classic study, *The Wandering People of God*. Now, however, we can see that the author of this epistle has not presented Christian existence in this manner out of a general desire to translate the gospel into terms that would be intelligible to Gentiles steeped in gnostic mythology, as Käsemann had thought.[58] Rather, this notion of being cut loose, without place, free, is the authentic religious response to the experience of alienation and dissatisfaction felt by so many early Christians, as well as by many others in Hellenistic antiquity who expressed their utopian ethos using various mythic schemes to imagine their eventual escape from this hostile world.

Of central importance in this utopian discourse was the question of sacrifice, the temple, the altar—the cultic tether that held everyone in place. That is why, in the face of adversity, suffering, even possible martyrdom, the author of Hebrews does not speak of faith only as endurance, but also as leave-taking.[59] The one who follows Christ follows him "outside the camp," away from the old sanctuary and its altar to a new city that is to come, with new sacrifices of a different sort:

> We have an altar from which those who officiate in the tent have no right to eat. For the bodies of those animals whose blood is brought into the sanctuary by the high priest as a sacrifice for sin are burned outside the camp. Therefore Jesus also suffered outside the city gate in order to sanctify the people by his own blood. Let us then go to him outside the camp and bear the abuse he endured. For here we have no lasting city, but we are looking for the city that is to come. (13:10-14)

Jesus died as a sacrifice that really was no sacrifice. His sacrificial death was in reality a brutal state execution. As such it became for

Jesus' followers the sacrifice to end all sacrifices. It became an event that would stand once and for all as the great threshold over which the followers of Jesus would pass out of the ordered world of their past, a world that had cast Jesus out, and into some unknown future. Jesus' fate took him out of the ordered world, the city, "outside the camp," into that great beyond of chaos and no-place. His followers now took this fate to be their own. Behind them lay the polis and its hearth, the empire and its gods, the Temple and its altar. Before them lay the mysterious journey into faith: a life of trusting God to bring them to some new and better place, a "city that is to come." Christ's death had freed them from both the tyranny and the security of place, to embrace in fear, trembling, and joy the prospects of no-place. So the unclean and unsettling death of Jesus became the sacrifice to end all sacrifice, and an invitation to take leave of one's home fires to seek life in the liberating and terrifying experience of no-place.

Epilogue

The Resurrection of a Nobody

And when we say also that the Word, who is the first-birth of God, was produced without sexual union, and that he, Jesus Christ, our Teacher, was crucified and died, and rose again, and ascended into heaven, we propound nothing different from what you believe regarding those who you esteem sons of Jupiter. For you know how many sons your esteemed writers ascribed to Jupiter: Mercury, the interpreting word and teacher of all; Aesclepius, who, though he was a great physician, was struck by a thunder bolt, and so ascended into heaven; and Bacchus too, after being torn limb from limb; and Hercules, when he had committed himself to the flames to escape his toils; and the sons of Leda, and Dioscuri; and Perseus, son of Danae; and Bellerophon, who, though sprung from mortals, rose to heaven on the horse Pegasus. And what shall I say of Ariadne, and those who, like her, have been declared to be set among the stars? And what of your emperors who die among yourselves, whom you deem worthy of deification, and in whose behalf you produce someone who swears he has seen the burning Caesar rise to heaven from the funeral pyre?
—Justin Martyr, *1 Apology* 21

When someone today begins to speak of "the resurrection," most of us will likely assume that it is Jesus' resurrection to which the speaker refers, not the resurrection of someone else. True, in the world of the tabloids one might find an occasional rival to *the* resurrection: an Elvis sighting, the face of the Virgin Mary on the side of a weathered building in Kansas. But it is usually no contest. "Jesus is risen!" is serious religion; "Elvis lives!" is not. This is not just because most of us find it slightly preposterous to elevate a rock-and-roll idol to divine status. Martin Luther King Jr., Ghandi, even Lou Gehrig could not give Jesus much serious competition today. *The* resurrection is unequivocally *Jesus'* resurrection for us. This is because most of us do not really believe in resurrection from the dead, except, of course, in the case of Jesus. He is in a class by himself. His resurrection is what makes him who he is: the unique, divine Son of God.

This way of thinking about the resurrection places us in a completely different frame of mind from those ancients who might have heard for the first time the claim that Jesus had been raised from the dead. Ancients, for the most part, had no trouble believing in resurrection per se. It was a common element of most ancient religions, and a fate thought to have been shared by many prophets, martyrs, and heroes. King, Ghandi, and Gehrig would have been good candidates by ancient standards. Jesus, on the other hand, was not. To most who had heard of him, he was not a prophet but a small-time pretender. His death was an execution, not a martyrdom. His life of poverty and his death in disgrace were far from heroic. Not much chance there for a godlike happy ending. Resurrection was not for nobodies.

A famous grafitto (see page 105) discovered in the mid-nineteenth century on the Palatine Hill in Rome illustrates the difference most strikingly.[1] The crude etching, meant as a joke, is of a man with the head of an ass hanging on a cross. Next to the cross a small boy kneels in adoration. An inscription reads: Alexamenos worships his God. A similar grafitto in an adjoining room identifies the boy, Alexamenos (perhaps a slave), as a Christian. Today the image is almost universally repelling. Then, difficult as it is to imagine, it was probably thought a pretty good joke. Elvis on a crucifix—that just about captures what "Jesus is risen!" might have sounded like to most respectable people of the ancient world.

For ancients, the Christian resurrection proclamation was not unique. When Justin Martyr wished to explain this aspect of Christian faith to the emperor, Antoninus Pius, in the second century, he had plenty of analogies to which he might refer. To be sure, the Christian

"Alexamenos worships his God." Reprinted from Rodolfo Lanciani, *Ancient Rome in the Light of Recent Discoveries* (Boston: Houghton Mifflin, 1888), 122.

accounts of Jesus' resurrection do have unique features, as do all particular religious narratives. But the basic idea that someone who had died might come back to life was not unique. Even in the New Testament itself Jesus' resurrection is not unique. Lazarus is raised from the dead in John 11, as is the unnamed daughter of Jairus in Mark 6:35-43. Paul sees Jesus' own resurrection not as a unique event, but as the first of many—"the first fruits of those who have fallen asleep" (1 Cor 15:20), as he puts it. In his account of Jesus' crucifixion, Matthew incorporates this end-time hope as the dead begin to come back to life already at the moment of Jesus' death, emerging from their tombs and to wander the city with him three days later (Matt 27:52-53). In the second century, Irenaeus does not blanch to claim that he and other Christian leaders could themselves raise the dead.[2] Ancients also believed in the resurrection of great heroes, all the "sons of Jupiter," and most importantly in the world of Christian origins, the resurrection and exaltation, or "apotheosis," of the emperor, welcomed to heaven at the end of his life as the divine son of God. In such a world, the hard part about the Christian resurrection proclamation would not have been believing in resurrection. The hard part would have been believing that Jesus, a nobody, had been raised from the dead.

Herein lies the great difference in the way ancients and moderns proclaim their faith in the risen Lord. For moderns, resurrection is impossible, except, of course, in the case of Jesus. It thus has become a unique event in our imagination, an event that proves we are right about Jesus, the Son of God. For ancients, resurrection is quite possible. It is what happens to sons of gods and heroes. But Jesus did not fit well into this fraternity. Ancients readily believed in resurrection; they just would not have thought Jesus to be a likely candidate. His death was not heroic. He was born a peasant and died a criminal. Yet his followers said of him what others said of Hercules, Aesclepius, or Caesar. Why?

The Meaning of Resurrection

To answer this question, we might turn first to the New Testament itself. Here we find the earliest surviving witness to the resurrection proclamation in one of Paul's letters, First Corinthians: "For I delivered to you as of first importance what I also received, that Christ died for our sins in accordance with the scriptures, that he was buried, that he was raised on the third day, in accordance with the scriptures" (1 Cor 15:3-4). This ancient tradition actually predates

Paul, as the phrase he uses to introduce it clearly indicates: Paul was taught this, and so now passes it on. Reference to "the scriptures" probably indicates the learned origins of the tradition. Someone has taken the time to reflect on Jesus' death and has decided that his death was the sort that carries meaning, the sort of death one finds discussed in Scripture.

Now, as in most cases where Paul makes use of Christian tradition, he is doing so here for the purpose of winning an argument. The nature of the argument in 1 Corinthians 15 is often misunderstood. The dispute was not over whether Jesus had been raised from the dead, as one might assume from the way such passages as 1 Corinthians 15:14 are used today, typically on an Easter Sunday morning: "if Christ has not been raised, then our preaching is in vain and your faith is in vain." This is misleading. No, the question Paul addresses has to do not with the fate of Jesus, but with the fate of others who have died: is there a *general* resurrection of the dead, or not? This is clear from Paul's opening salvo in the debate: "Now if Christ is preached as raised from the dead, how can some of you say that there is no resurrection of the dead?" (15:12). The logic of his argument in the verses to come will unfold as follows: "If you all agree that Jesus has been raised from the dead—and you do, don't you?—then you have to agree that there will also be a general resurrection of the dead." As Paul says in verse 20: "But in fact Christ has been raised from the dead, the first fruits of those who have fallen asleep." His resurrection is not unique, but the first of many that are to come.

The reason why some in Paul's Corinthian churches were denying the general resurrection is disputed. It may be that they thought in baptism they had already been transformed into the immortals they were destined to be. The resurrection, in their understanding, had already taken place in baptism.[3] Paul's own ideas on the meaning of baptism are suggestive of this view (see especially Romans 6).[4] Or it may be that this dispute was simply the result of ethnic diversity within the Pauline communities. Greeks and Romans believed in the resurrection of certain extraordinary individuals, but not in a general resurrection. In any event, not believing in the future resurrection of the dead left the community with a problem: what happens when someone dies? Inadvertently, Paul may have already answered this question, if in Corinth he had said something akin to what he would later say in his letter to the Romans: "the wages of sin is death" (Rom 6:23; cf. 5:12, 21). On such a view, death could be seen quite easily as punishment for sin. The person who dies before Christ's return is only confirmed as a sinner, not worthy of the empire of God after all. That this is what some in Corinth did indeed believe is suggested by Paul's words in 1 Corinthians 15:29a: "Otherwise what do people mean by being baptized on behalf of the dead?" Apparently some of the Corinthians thought that even after the wages of sin had been earned, surrogate baptism could save the dead person from his or her fate.[5] Of course, Paul knew that he now had these surrogate baptizers in checkmate: if the dead are truly dead and gone, for what, or how, could baptism really save them? "If the dead are not raised at all, why are people being baptized on their behalf" (15:29b)? For the dead to enjoy the fruits of surrogate baptism they would have to come back to life at some point in the future. God would have to raise them from the dead.

But this little trick of an answer is not the main thrust of Paul's argument in 1 Corinthians 15. His real argument is that Christ has been raised from the dead—something to which all the Corinthians would certainly agree. This was the content of the preaching and witness Paul had brought to them to begin with. But if, as they now seemed to believe, "there is no resurrection of the dead," then one must also say that "Christ has not been raised," and Paul's preaching was in vain, and their faith too (15:13-14). But why should these things be so linked? Why, if there is no resurrection to come, must one also say that Christ has not been raised? Remember, for Paul the resurrection of Jesus was not a unique event. Jesus was the "first fruits of those who have fallen asleep." The resurrection of Jesus, for Paul, was part of a great, unfolding cosmic drama in which the powers of the world were being overthrown. Paul writes:

> For as by a mortal came death, by a mortal also has come the res-
> urrection of the dead. For as in Adam all die, so also in Christ
> shall all be made to live. But each in his own order: Christ the first
> fruits, then at his coming those who belong to Christ. Then
> comes the end, when he delivers the kingdom to God the Father
> after destroying every rule and every authority and every power.
> For he must reign until he has put all his enemies under his feet.
> The last enemy to be destroyed is death. (15:21-26)

Paul's framing of the resurrection proclamation within an apocalyptic scenario reminds us where the idea of resurrection comes from
in the Jewish tradition. Both resurrection and apocalypticism address
the same fundamental issue: What happens when life and death do
not bear witness to good and evil?[6] When the evil live, and the good
die, where is God? Does God care? As Jews suffered endlessly under a
succession of foreign rulers with no apparent sign that faithfulness to
the God of their ancestors could bear any fruit at all, prophets and
visionaries raised a cry, a protest to the injustice they knew in this
world. "Mortal, can these bones live?" God asks the prophet Ezekiel
(Ezek 37:3). Out of the genocidal experience of exile comes the
prophet's stunning vision of the dry bones of the house of Israel coming together again, "bone to its bone . . . sinews . . . flesh . . . and skin"
(Ezek 37:7-8). By the will of God the bodies of all those slain, now laying silent in the valley of the dry bones, are reconstituted, reassem-
bled, and finally resuscitated to live again: "Thus says the Lord GOD:
'Come from the four winds, O breath, and breathe upon these slain,
that they may live.' And I prophesied as God commanded me, and the
breath came into them, and they lived, and stood on their feet, a vast
multitude" (Ezek 37:9). With a word from the prophet, the hope and
promise of a just and merciful God is given new life.

Ezekiel was not alone. Isaiah, too, found hope in the idea of resurrection (Isaiah 24–27). Later, as Jews suffered under a series of foreign
rulers, the idea of resurrection became a varied but constant element
in the Jewish response to the experience of evil and injustice in the
world. One finds it in Daniel (12:1-3) and the early Enoch literature

(*1 Enoch* 22–27) from the third century B.C.E., and in the later Enoch material (*1 Enoch* 92–105), *Jubilees* (23:11-31), and Second Maccabees (chap. 7, passim), all from the second century B.C.E. Closer to the period of Christian origins, it appears in the Wisdom of Solomon (chaps. 1-6, passim), Baruch (chaps. 49–51), and 4 Ezra (chap. 7). The idea that God would someday intervene in one last great cosmic battle, raise the righteous dead, and destroy their enemies was at home among a people who suffered long under brutal foreign rule. In chapter 2, I dwelt at some length on the effect of this legacy, as found especially in Fourth Maccabees, on the development of the early Christian idea that Jesus died as a martyr, true to his cause. The martyr's story, with its final chapter of vindication, became the narrative home of resurrection in the Christian story, as it had been among Jews for centuries. It is this rich tradition to which the creed Paul cites in 1 Corinthians 15:3-4 refers when it declares that Christ died, was buried, and was raised on the third day "in accordance with the scriptures."

Paul knew this tradition and the experience that made it relevant, as did many early followers of Jesus. Paul had spent time in a Roman prison and apparently had his own brushes with martyrdom. For him, the resurrection (first of Jesus, then of all who belong to Christ) was the assurance that his own attempts to live a life faithful to the cause of Jesus were not in vain. And if it were not so? "Why am I in peril every hour? . . . I die every day! What do I gain if, humanly speaking, I fought with beasts at Ephesus? If the dead are not raised, 'Let us eat and drink, for tomorrow we die'" (1 Cor 15:30-32).

Throughout 1 Corinthians 15 Paul talks the talk of the martyr. Those who have died, and who risk death, will not be lost. This is the importance of resurrection. His concept of the resurrection is bodily. This was very important in view of the martyr's experience of suffering. The martyrological literature dwells on the physical pain of torture, on the vulnerability of the body, and on the need to rise above the dread of what one's enemies can do to one's body. [7] For the martyr, release from the vulnerable, physical body and the restoration of that body, but now in an invulnerable, imperishable form, would be the very definition of salvation. So Paul says of the resurrection of the bodies of those who have died, following the analogy of the sown seed: "What is sown is perishable, what is raised is imperishable. It is sown in dishonor, it is raised in glory. It is sown in weakness, it is raised in power. It is sown a physical body, it is raised a spiritual body" (1 Cor 15:42-44).

Paul's concept of the resurrection is *bodily*, but *not physical*. Jesus and those who are to follow him in resurrection have "spiritual bodies," not physical bodies. For the martyr this is crucial. This is how the torturer's power, the power of death, is broken. When the martyr sheds the physical body to put on the spiritual body, he or she is freed from the vulnerability that comes with physical existence. The torturer's iron cannot touch a spiritual body. So Paul says, quoting that great restoration text, Isaiah 25, "Death is swallowed up in victory," and then, twisting Hosea's words of vengeance into a martyr's victory chant: "O death, where is your victory? O death, where is your sting?" (1 Cor 15:54b-55).

Jesus' resurrection, as the first of all who would follow after him, was the assurance that his life and the lives of those who, like Paul, found themselves in the perilous position of being a dissident in the Roman Empire were not without purpose. Indeed, they believed that their lives carried God's own purpose for a new world lived out in rebellion against the old. Should the old world still prevail against them, they believed that redemption awaited them beyond the suffering they might temporarily endure in this life. Jesus was a martyr. He died for the righteous cause of God's new empire. To say that God raised him from the dead was to say that his cause was indeed just, that his empire was truly God's empire. "Jesus is risen" finally means "Jesus was right."[8]

The only remarkable thing about these thoughts—and it is truly remarkable—is that someone thought them about *Jesus*. One might well think them about the heroic brothers and their brave mother of Maccabean fame, whose public witness was nothing less than astonishing. One might well think them about a better-known figure, like John the Baptist, who stood up to kings and humiliated the powerful. Most loyal subjects of the empire would have thought such thoughts about the emperors, especially Julius Caesar and his adopted son, Augustus. Julius was martyred; Augustus was the hero who avenged his death and established peace once again. Here were God's true sons, sent to bring peace and prosperity to the whole world. The *Pax Romana* itself bore witness to their authenticity.

But what of Jesus? He was no hero. He led no armies. He inspired no rebellion. The following he attracted was small and comprised people of the lowest station, marginal in their shame and dirt—expendables. He was executed as a criminal of the lowest sort, without heroic struggle or a moving speech to ignite his followers. Crucifixion offered no honor. He died quickly, a sign of weakness. What is remarkable about the early Christian resurrection proclamation was that it claimed *Jesus* had been raised from the dead—Jesus, not Caesar.

Resurrection Proves Nothing

So how did earliest Christians come to believe in the resurrection of Jesus? How did the followers of Jesus come to believe that he was a martyr, that his cause was just, and that they too should give themselves over to that cause, in spite of the dangers it posed? For many theologians and historians of early Christianity, the answer to this lies in the resurrection itself. For them, the resurrection of Jesus was that singularly astonishing event that convinced his followers they had been right about him all along. Had it not been for the resurrection, it is argued, they all would have given up and gone home, discouraged and disappointed. In short, without the resurrection, there would have been no Christianity.[9] But I am not convinced by this.

The evidence for the resurrection of Jesus is by itself not very compelling. It may seem compelling to Christians today, but this is only because our tradition has taught us to regard everything in the Bible as beyond question. It is also because most of us do not have much at stake in believing in the resurrection of Jesus. Martyrdom is not an issue for us. Precisely the opposite is more the case. We are encouraged and rewarded by our church and our culture for believing in the resurrection of Jesus. But what if believing in Jesus meant leaving house and home and risking a dissident lifestyle that could very well place one in mortal danger with the empire? What if it meant challenging the values of a culture that did not bear dissent with calm accepting? Would the early Christian resurrection proclamation have been enough to convince one that all these sacrifices were indeed worthwhile? I doubt it.

Paul's way of thinking about the resurrection was particularly problematic. He insisted that the dead will be raised as "spirits," that they will have "spiritual bodies," not physical bodies (1 Cor 15:35-58). Further, he thought of the risen Jesus himself as a spirit, experienced internally in moments of ecstasy, as in that moment when God chose "to reveal his son *in* me" (Gal 1:16), as Paul says.[10] From then on, Paul thought of himself as coming under Christ's control, of being "in Christ," even of having "the mind of Christ." To the sophisticated ancient observer of Christianity what Paul was experiencing was a simple and common case of spirit possession. To speak of Christ as a spirit, a *pneuma*, was to speak of him not as a god but as a mere ghost, doomed to wander the earth like so many other tortured souls of criminals who met with a similar violent end.[11] To outsiders, Paul's Christianity might have seemed to be nothing more than vulgar grave religion.[12] Paul's experience of the Spirit of Christ convinced him only because it was his own experience, quite real and very powerful.

The author of the Gospel of Mark was probably aware that outsiders could arrive at such a negative view of the Christian resurrection proclamation. This is perhaps why he takes at least two resurrection appearance stories and treats them as though they were not. The transfiguration of Jesus (Mark 9:2-8) is the better known of these, probably a mountaintop postresurrection appearance story originally.[13] The other is embedded in the story of Jesus walking on water in Mark 6:48-50.[14] This one in particular reads like a ghost story. As Jesus appears mysteriously walking across the waves in the dim wee hours of the morning, the disciples scream, for "they thought it was a ghost" (v. 49). Mark was probably leery of this, or any spooky postmortem appearance stories, and steered clear of them altogether. Instead, he presents the witness of the empty tomb (Mark 16:1-8). To Christians accustomed to finding epiphanies of Jesus at the end of their Gospels, this abrupt ending to Mark may seem rather incomplete. But Mark's empty tomb story would have appealed more widely to readers in the Jewish and Hellenistic world, who would have heard similar stories told of heroes who had been rescued from dire straits and translated directly to heaven to live in safety with the gods.[15] In Mark's Gospel Jesus becomes a respectable hero, saved from his foes in a surprise ending—a miraculous escape.

But, of course, an empty tomb is hardly definitive proof, even for the mildest of skeptics. In the Gospel of Matthew the chief priests are made to offer the obvious retort: "Tell people, 'His disciples came by night and stole him away while we were asleep'" (Matt 28:13). In the Gospel of John even Mary succumbs to this conclusion when, after discovering the tomb empty, she encounters Jesus in the garden but does not recognize him. Instead she complains to him, thinking that he is the gardener in charge: "they have taken away my Lord, and I do not know where they have laid him" (John 20:13). An empty tomb is really nothing but a missing body in need of an explanation: stolen or raised from the dead?

The solution to this problem, of course, is to produce the body— alive. This is what Luke does by adding a particularly graphic appearance story to Mark's earlier narrative. In Luke the risen Jesus appears not as a mysterious spiritual presence, as with Paul, but as a living, breathing, *eating* body:

> As they were saying this, Jesus himself stood among them. But they were startled and frightened, and supposed that they saw a ghost (*pneuma*). And he said to them, "Why are you troubled, and why do questions arise in your hearts? See my hands and my

feet, that it is I myself; touch me and see; for a ghost (*pneuma*) does not have flesh and bones as you see that I have." And when he had said this he showed them his hands and his feet. And while they still disbelieved, out of joy, and marveled, he said to them, "Do you have anything here to eat?" They gave him a piece of broiled fish, and he took it and ate it in front of them. (Luke 24:36-43)

One might suppose that Luke, with this "eat the fish" test, has finally settled the matter of whether Jesus was a mere ghost or a true hero. "Touch me and see, for a ghost does not have flesh and bones as I have." Without those flesh and bones Luke must think that the broiled fish would have fallen directly onto the floor! But with this story Luke has probably crossed the thin line, even for ancients, dividing the sublime from the ridiculous. Luke has also wandered about as far as one can get from Paul, who insisted most adamantly, "flesh and blood cannot inherit the empire of God!" (1 Cor 15:50).

If John the evangelist had known Luke's story, he would not have liked it. He knew that in the heat of conflict and under the pressure of threat to life and livelihood, such proofs are not satisfactory. His arch-skeptic, Thomas, voices the outer limit to which such ridiculous demands might stretch: "Unless I . . . place my finger in the mark of the nails, and place my hand in his side, I will not believe" (John 20:25). Presently Jesus appears and gives Thomas the opportunity to do just that. "Put your finger here, and see my hands; and stick out your hand and put it in my side. Don't be an unbeliever, be a believer!" taunts the Johannine Christ (20:27). The ridiculous has now become the macabre, as John parodies the attempt to prove what he knows must be accepted and believed on entirely different grounds. "Have you believed because you have seen me? Blessed are those who have not seen, and yet still believe" (20:29). Jesus' scolding of Thomas is really aimed at the many in John's community who longed for a sign, a miracle, anything to see them through the dire times in which they were living. But it is in such times that the flimsiness of faith based on miraculous proofs is easily exposed.

The followers of Jesus needed more than a miracle. Miracles were a dime a dozen in the ancient world, and resurrection was part of every ancient religious tradition. For the followers of Jesus, believing in the miracle of God raising someone from the dead was not a problem. The problem was believing that God would raise *Jesus* from the dead.

Why Did They Believe?

Why, then, did the friends and followers of Jesus believe that God had raised him from the dead? If sightings of the risen Lord would not have convinced the unconvinced, nor empty tombs, nor fantastic stories of a fish-eating, perforated, bodily Christ, what then would have convinced the followers of Jesus that he was not dead, but raised by the God of their ancestors and taken up into heaven to live on, seated at the right hand of God?

As we have seen, in the Jewish tradition the presupposition for any claims that God had raised someone from the dead was not the appearance of the departed in ghostly form, the discovery of an empty tomb, or any other such postmortem proof that God had chosen to intervene against the forces that killed him. Resurrection, as vindication, presupposed only that one of God's righteous ones had been slain in faithfulness to God. This is how the followers of Jesus felt about him. These were the few who heard his words as God's Word, who experienced his deeds as epiphanic. We might find it hard to imagine that something like the first beatitude could inspire that kind of loyalty and devotion. Perhaps one would have to be a beggar to know how splendid those words sound: "Blessed are beggars, for yours is the empire of God." Perhaps one would have to experience the interminable loneliness of the permanently unclean to know how powerful and transforming a simple invitation to table could be. Perhaps only an enslaved prostitute could experience gracious acceptance and the offer of freedom so powerfully that death could seem utterly irrelevant to its continuing effect. For these few friends and followers, Jesus was a hero of no less stature than Eleazar, the slain priest of Fourth Maccabees. He was their Elijah, their Moses, their Adam. They believed in him thus, not because of his resurrection. They believed in him thus because of the way he touched their lives. And because he had touched their lives in this profound way, they believed in his resurrection.

One of the earliest forms of the resurrection proclamation is a simple formula (actually three different forms), repeated several times in Paul's letters, that speaks of God as the one who "raises Jesus from the dead."[16] This turns out to be a very Jewish way of speaking about God in the period of early Judaism. In the traditional Jewish liturgy, which likely derives from the period of Christian origins, the second of the Eighteen Benedictions says, "Blessed are you, Yahweh, who makes the dead to live." This is not very far from that simple early Christian formula; indeed, Paul seems to quote the second benediction itself in Rom 4:17, praising the God of Abraham, "who gives life to the dead."[17] The parallel is suggestive. Let us imagine a gathering of Jesus' early followers sometime not long after his death. Jesus sponsored such gatherings in his lifetime, probably around a meal, and so his followers would have continued on in his memory, gathering for meals and to share stories of Jesus then, and life now. There would have been blessings and traditional prayers offered around the loose structure of a meal, eventually a prayer for the bread and a prayer for the wine. Among them someone like Paul could well have heard something like: "Blessed are you, Yahweh, who raised Jesus from the dead." To the prayers would have been added a hymn, perhaps the hymn Paul records in correspondence to the Philippian church (Phil 2:6-11), whose middle verses went something like,

> And being found in human form,
>   he humbled himself
> and became obedient until death, even death on a cross.
> Therefore God has highly exalted him,
>   and given him the name that is above every name . . .
>   Lord Jesus Christ.

The extraordinary christological claims that appear in this traditional, pre-Pauline hymn to Christ are not predicated on stories of an
empty tomb or miraculous appearances. The song proceeds directly
from death to exaltation, and the only prerequisite for this giant leap
is "obedience until death." This is martyrological language thrust
into song.[18] The followers of Jesus first proclaimed his resurrection in
celebration of his life.

Jesus was a visionary who attracted a loyal following. He had a
cause, the empire of God. All those who followed him believed in this
cause and in him, one of God's righteous ones. If the enemy were to
find and kill him, his followers would have believed with all their
hearts that the God of their ancestors, the God of justice and righteousness, would redeem him from suffering and restore him to life.
They believed God would raise him from the dead because they
believed in him. It did not matter to them that he was a nobody. They
were themselves nobodies and outsiders. Jesus was a nobody who
convinced them that they were somebody to God. This nobody was
their hero, their prophet, *their* "son of Jupiter." This is why, when at
last he was killed, they proclaimed his resurrection. They could have
done this on the day he died, and probably did.

Did Anything Really Happen?

But in addition to the martyrological talk, Paul also speaks to the
Corinthians of other, more mysterious things—of "appearances": "he
appeared to Cephas, then to the twelve. Then he appeared to more than
five hundred brothers and sisters at one time, most of whom are still
alive, though some have fallen asleep. Then he appeared to James, then
to all the apostles. Last of all, as to one untimely born, he appeared also
to me" (1 Cor 15:5-8). What shall we make of this tradition? Did Jesus
really appear to Peter, James, other of his followers, and even to five hundred people at one time? Did such things happen, or was this simply
the tradition taking shape around certain figures of authority?[19]

I think that this tradition represents something that did happen, but probably not something so clear and unambiguous as one might conclude from Paul's manner of expression in 1 Corinthians 15. To understand this tradition we should probably begin with Jesus himself, and the sort of experiences he and his followers had during his lifetime. Jesus was a "spirit person," to quote Marcus Borg.[20] The movement he began was probably one in which ecstatic religious experiences—experiences of the Spirit—were important and defining. Jesus himself was an exorcist, an activity in antiquity normally involving the manipulation of spirits, or being manipulated by them.[21] The tradition of Jesus' baptism links his status as a Son of God to the descent of the Spirit upon him, an idea that persisted into the Pauline churches, where followers of Jesus possessed by the Holy Spirit cried out "Abba," thus testifying to the fact that they too were children of God (Rom 8:14-16; Gal 4:6-7). These passages and a host of others from Paul's letters, the Gospels, and Acts give a clear picture of the early Jesus movement also as a spiritually charged religious following. The followers of Jesus continued to have ecstatic religious experiences after his death, just as they had had them before.

What did they make of these spiritual experiences? Paul's references to them are instructive. Sometimes Paul speaks of the work of "the Spirit." Sometimes he speaks of the work of "God's Spirit," the "Holy Spirit," the "Spirit of Life," or the "Spirit of the Lord." And sometimes he speaks of the work of the "Spirit of Christ."[22] The following passage from Romans, in which Paul discusses this life in the Spirit, illustrates just how interchangeable all of these terms are for Paul:

> But you are not of the flesh; you are in the Spirit, since the Spirit of God dwells in you. Anyone who does not have the Spirit of Christ does not belong to him. But if Christ is in you, though the body is dead because of sin, the Spirit is life because of righteousness. If the Spirit of the one who raised Jesus from the dead dwells in you, the one who raised Christ from the dead will give life to your mortal bodies also through his Spirit that dwells in you. (Rom 8:9-11)

For Paul the Spirit is the Spirit of Christ is the Spirit of God is the Spirit "that dwells in you." It is this Spirit that gives them life, that "is life."

The spiritual life that Jesus cultivated with his followers before his death did not cease to exist when he died. It continued. Only now, his followers could speak of this spiritual activity not simply as God's Spirit moving among them, but as Christ's Spirit, or the "Spirit of his Son" (Gal 4:6). Why? Because it was through Jesus, their Christ, that they had first come to experience God in this new way. Now, as they continued to experience the Spirit of God after Jesus' death, they would name it also as they had first discovered it, as the Spirit of Christ. This is how I would understand Paul's statement in 1 Corinthians 15 that on one occasion more than five hundred people had experienced the risen Christ at the same time. This probably does not refer to a gigantic Jesus appearing before a crowd of hundreds. It refers to spiritual ecstasy, experienced by many in the act of gathering for worship. These moments of spiritual ecstasy, experienced individually and in communal worship, now became experiences of the risen Christ. For many, they became the defining experience in following Jesus, so much so that Luke, in Acts, offers a stylized depiction of this sort of ecstatic, spiritual experience as the thing that gave birth to Christianity itself (Acts 2:1-13). Perhaps in the inner dimensions of the spiritual lives of figures like James and Peter, who had been particularly close to Jesus, these experiences took on the more personal character of an encounter with their former teacher and friend, his tortured body now transformed and freed from his former suffering. These "appearances" of Jesus became for them the reauthorization for continuing what he had begun, their apostolic mandate.

A Matter of Decision

When all is said and done, of course, the spiritual experiences of ancient Christians do not prove that Jesus was raised from the dead or that he was the Son of God. For ancients these things might just as easily have been dismissed as ghost stories. Moderns might speak of them as mass hysteria, or as the grief experience of seeing again a loved one who has recently died, as happens quite commonly today. The ambiguity of these experiences underscores once again the fact that Christian faith does not really have its origins in such experiences. Rather, the followers of Jesus spoke of their ecstatic religious experiences in this way—as experiences of the risen Jesus—because of a conviction whose origins must be traced back to another beginning. Their conviction about him began on a day long before his death, on an afternoon, or a morning, when, out of the blue, they heard Jesus say something, or saw him do something that moved them, deeply. In his company they came to know God. In his words they heard the Word of God. In his activity they experienced the empire of God. They became committed to him and his vision of a new empire, a new world coming into being. They believed in him. When he died, they knew that the Spirit of God they had experienced in his words and deeds was not thereby snuffed out. Their Jewish tradition of martyrdom and redemption gave them the words by which to proclaim this: God raised Jesus from the dead. Now, as the spiritual life of the community of his followers continued, they could speak of it not just as the life of the Spirit, or of God's Spirit. It now became also life in the Spirit of Christ.

The followers of Jesus did not believe in him because of the resurrection. They believed in the resurrection because they first believed in him and in the spiritual life he unleashed among them.[23] This is, finally, what the resurrection proclamation is about. It is about the decision to believe in Jesus and to give oneself over to the Spirit to be discovered in his life.

Killing Jesus (A Conclusion)

*Christ crucified rules, and it may be that the true business of
modern Christianity is to crucify him again and again so that
he can never get a word out of his mouth.*
—Barbara Ehrenreich, *Nickel and Dimed*

When Jesus was killed by authorities charged with keeping the Roman *Pax*, his friends and followers were not without cultural resources for dealing with the violent end of his life. As they began to reflect on Jesus' death, they soon came to see it not as a tragedy or calamity, but as an inevitable part of his life, an end fitting of the kind of life Jesus led. They began to develop ways of speaking of the death of Jesus that would connect it with his life and draw attention to his life as decisive for their own lives.

One way that these early followers of Jesus could speak of his death was simply as the death of a victim—a victim of Roman imperial power, a dissident to the great Roman vision of a single empire encompassing the whole known world, standing alone, without rival or alternative. They knew that to be a follower of Jesus was to embrace the foolishness of raising a dissident voice and an alternative vision to the Roman *Pax*. "We proclaim a crucified Messiah," says Paul, who is both the "power of God" and the "wisdom of God" (1 Cor 1:23-24). Power that is weakness; wisdom that is foolishness—these were the realities that determined Paul's new life in being a follower of Jesus. To be a follower of Jesus was to become a "fool for Christ's sake." It meant embracing weakness, not strength; shame rather than honor. It meant welcoming vilification, persecution, and slander. It meant becoming "the refuse of the world, the offscouring of all things" (1 Cor 4:8-13). As Jesus' dissident life led to his death as a victim of imperial power, so also many of his followers led dissident lives that in turn earned them the fate of victim as well.

But the followers of Jesus soon began to speak of his death not simply as the death of a victim, but as the glorious death of a martyr. The rich and varied Jewish martyrological tradition was perhaps the most fertile and productive interpretive field for early Christians. From it come the idea that Jesus' death was a sacrifice, and the belief that God could, and would, raise Jesus from the dead. But the direction in which the martyrdom tradition points is not forward, into the heavenly future life the martyr is said to enjoy, but backward, to the way of life, the values, and the cause for which the martyr was willing to die. The martyr's death is a witness—a witness to the ultimate value of the cause for which he or she died, and a witness to the way of faithfulness to that cause, a way that may well lead to death. The martyr must be willing to pay the ultimate price for the convictions she or he holds. But before one might be willing to die for a cause, one must first be willing to live for it. Thus the New Testament Gospels, all of which make use of the martyrological tradition, present Jesus' life not simply as a prelude to his death, but as the *way of life* one must embrace as one follows Jesus to the cross.

This was true of Paul as well—though this is often obscured by the fact that Paul very seldom discusses Jesus' life and only occasionally makes use of his words. But of all the characters that appear in the New Testament, it is Paul who emulates the life of Jesus most thoroughly. If Mark's fictive rich young ruler turns away from Jesus when he learns of the rigors of renunciation Jesus requires, Paul did not. Paul took up the life of Jesus and made it his own. This he says of his own struggles with life as a dissident voice in the empire: "we are always carrying in the body the death of Jesus, so that the life of Jesus might be made manifest in our body; for in living we are always given up to death for Jesus' sake, so that the life of Jesus might be made manifest in our mortal flesh" (2 Cor 4:10-11). For Paul and others who came to understand Jesus' death as a martyrdom, embracing his death was really about embracing his *life*. The martyr's death means nothing apart from the life to which it bears witness. This is why for generations the Jesus movement would be known simply as "the way." Following Jesus meant embracing his way of life.

Finally, the followers of Jesus also spoke of his death as a sacrifice. To speak thus may seem at first glance finally to take leave of Jesus' life and to draw his death into theological abstraction. A sacrificial lamb is born to die, nothing more. But this was not how the early followers of Jesus made use of the metaphor of sacrifice to interpret his death. The idea that a *person* might become a sacrifice for sin originally came out of the martyrdom tradition. In the Maccabean literature, for example, it is because of the martyr's extraordinary faithfulness to God that his or her death might be regarded by God as atonement for the sins of the people. It is the martyr's extraordinary life and faithfulness unto death that finally turns God's anger, and stirs God to come at last to rescue the suffering people of God. Ironically, in the New Testament it is Caiaphas in John's Gospel who gives clearest expression to this idea: "do you not understand that it is expedient for you that one man should die for the people, and that the whole nation should not perish" (John 11:50).

But even when the idea of Jesus' death as a sacrifice was not explicitly tied to the martyrological tradition from whence it came, it remained connected to Jesus' life in a very creative way. As Jesus' followers pondered his death as a sacrifice, and considered this within the context of a culture in which sacrifice was the glue that held every stick of the social infrastructure firmly in place, they began to see how Jesus' death could function cultically to free them from that infrastructure, and their cultically sanctioned places in it. Like the sacrifices that held together family, clan, city, and empire, they found that their common meals—sacrificial meals, as all meals were—could become a place of new identity and new social formation. And as they began to walk away from the sacrificial fires that held the old world together, they discovered once again the freedom to become something new in this new microsociety, "the body of Christ," held together by the sacrifice of Jesus' own body. At these new tables—altars—where slaves and prostitutes sat as equals with merchants, scholars, and even the occasional state official, they received a new identity and purpose. But this was exactly what people had experienced in the table fellowship of Jesus himself. Jesus gathered at table the clean and the unclean, those with honor and those with none, prostitutes, sinners, beggars, and thieves. Around those tables all became equals, members of a common family, heirs to a new empire, the empire of God. After his death, as the tables of the Jesus movement became the altars around which a new society was formed, this process of personal and communal transformation continued. Thus what Jesus had meant to people in life was translated into a cultic parlance, and enacted once again through the appropriation of his death as a sacrifice.

And what of Jesus' resurrection? Here, at last, do we not finally take leave of his life? Is not the resurrection a thing of a different class altogether, an event so powerful and transforming that nothing in Jesus' life could carry much significance after that? Not at all. On the contrary, apart from Jesus' life the resurrection proclamation would never have been ventured in the first place. If we were to take the Gospel accounts of the resurrection as historical, they would not be convincing to anyone outside the inner circle of Jesus' devoted companions—and even some of them express doubts in these stories. I do not regard them as historical, but I do imagine that people in the Jesus movement did indeed have the kind of spiritual experiences Paul and others came to understand as postresurrection manifestations of the risen Christ. But why did they understand them thus? Why did they not see these powerful spiritual experiences as instances of spirit possession—as the ghost of Jesus coming back to haunt them, like so many other criminals and victims of violence and betrayal? Why did they say "God has raised Jesus from the dead?"

They said this because they had faith in Jesus. Those who said it first had known him. They believed in him and in his cause. To them, he was a martyr, not just a victim. In the ancient Jewish context of Christian origins, resurrection is part of the martyr's story. Resurrection is vindication. Could God raise Jesus from the dead? Any ancient would have answered yes to that question. But *would* God raise Jesus from the dead? To this question, only his followers could answer yes. And they said yes to it because they believed that Jesus' life had revealed him to be one of God's righteous ones. They believed that in his words were God's Word. They believed that in his deeds, Jesus had done the will of God. Resurrection, too, was a way of proclaiming the significance of Jesus' life.

I have become convinced that in each of these ways of interpreting Jesus' death, the followers of Jesus were in fact drawing attention to his *life*. His death mattered to them because his life had mattered to them. They spoke of his death in ways that affirmed his life, and reaffirmed their own commitment to the values and vision stamped into his life by his words and deeds. In his life, they had come to know God. To the followers and friends of Jesus, his death was important in its particularity—as the fate of him who said and did certain things, who stood for something so important to him that he was willing to give his life for it. That something was the vision of life he called the empire of God. They too believed in this vision of a new empire. If this vision was indeed *God's* empire, then the bearer of this vision was not dead. No executioner could kill what he was. To kill Jesus, you would have to kill the vision. This is what the cross could not do.

When Christian believers and theologians approach the question of Jesus' death today, these are generally not the concerns that lie close to hand. The things Jesus said that lead to his death are not at issue. What he lived or died for is of no concern. The event of Jesus' death has lost its particularity, its connection to the course of real human events that brought it about. In this abstracted status, Jesus' death has become for us a mythic event connected to the universal problem of death and the mysterious and frightening end of human life. As we fret over the moral and ethical failures of our lives and dread the perils and punishments that might lie beyond the grave, we are comforted by the knowledge that Jesus died "to save us from our sins." His resurrection assures us of our own immortality. If Jesus came to fulfill his cosmic destiny and die on the cross so that we might be saved, then anything else he might have done in his life—his own aspirations, his own values and vision, his carefully chosen words and daring prophetic deeds—pales by comparison. Ethics are never as important as salvation. With salvation it is life itself that hangs in the balance, our lives, which we desperately seek to preserve, even in the face of death, whose threat confronts us all. Thus Jesus' death and resurrection have become the universal saving events in which we find God's graciousness extended even to us, hopeless sinners, who have no intention of giving up the lives we live, oblivious to the vision of human life Jesus espoused and the God he embodied.

The eclipse of Jesus' death and resurrection in their particularity, and their elevation to the status of mythic events in a cosmic struggle, is invited perhaps by the way Paul and other early Christians placed Jesus' death and resurrection at the center of their own traditional apocalyptic hopes. Apocalypticism casts the struggle between good and evil in terms of a great cosmic battle, with the forces of God arrayed against the armies of the evil one. In Jewish apocalypticism the power and victory of God is marked by the resurrection of all those who have been slain by the forces of evil. In the final struggle their faithfulness and sufferings are vindicated. This is the framework in which Paul interpreted the resurrection of Jesus: he was the first-fruits, the first of those countless ones slain in the struggle against evil to come back to life (1 Cor 15:20). The resurrection was for Paul a signal, a cosmic alarm clock sounding the arrival of the final battle, which would begin any day. But Paul and others who interpreted Jesus' death and resurrection in this way did not detach the death and resurrection of Jesus from his life. The cosmic battle they believed they were witnessing was being waged over a specific idea, a real cause. The struggle in which they were engaged was the struggle for the vision of human life their crucified Messiah had espoused. For Paul, to experience the resurrection of Jesus was to become possessed by his Spirit, to share "the mind of Christ," and to embrace the life of Christ as his own. Paul and others formed communities that would be the "body of Christ," embodying the life of love and mutual care that Jesus had died for. What he died for, they would now live for, until God would finally establish the empire of God as the universal rule of love and justice in the world.

As time passed, however, and that first generation of friends and followers who had known Jesus and actually remembered his life passed from the scene, the connection between the particulars of Jesus' life and the mythic structures of cosmic battle became ever more tenuous and eventually were lost. The struggle became less and less a struggle for a particular set of values connected to Jesus, and more a clash of powers. The power of Christ was pitted against the religion of the Jews, against the pagan gods, and ultimately against the universal foe, death itself. One can see this already in the Apostles' Creed, where the life of Jesus has been diminished to a mere comma, a blank space residing quietly between "born of the Virgin Mary" and "suffered under Pontius Pilate." The elements of the Christian creed are the elements of the cosmic drama common to many ancient religious traditions: miraculous birth, death, resurrection, ascension. Jesus became simply another of the many dying-rising savior gods of antiquity, association with whom would assure safety in this world and the next. His table fellowship would for some become a mere dispensary for the "drug of immortality," the *pharmakon athanasias*, as Ignatius would come to speak of the communion bread (*Ephesians* 20).

Jesus Christ would eventually become the greatest Savior-God of all. His cross would become a logo, a talisman emblazoned on the shield of Constantine and his soldiers to protect them in battle. Jesus became a partisan, whose name would strike fear in the heart of anyone who by chance had not been born under his sign. In the Middle Ages his cross would become a sign of terror, before which Jews and Muslims would cringe in supplication, begging mercy from marauding hordes of crusaders, or stand in defiance only to be slain. The symbol of weakness Paul embraced became the symbol of merciless power, where it remains today for many Christian believers. One can see this still in its infinitely trivialized American form on any given Sunday afternoon—where the warriors of sport pause to cross themselves as a solemn prelude to the touchdown victory dance that is sure to follow, taunting those poor unfortunates inexplicably abandoned by Jesus in their moment of greatest need. Today the cross is for winners, not losers.

Is Jesus dead? Not yet. But what the cross could not do, Christians could. We are killing Jesus. Jesus was a sage, or if one prefers, a prophet. Sages and prophets live by their words and deeds. In this sense, for most of us who assemble in the name of Jesus, he is dead. His words and deeds mean little to us, if anything at all. We do not look to Jesus for a way of life, but for salvation. "He died that we might live." Indeed. It seems we have to kill him in order that we might live whatever lives our power and privilege will allow us to lead. When real life is at stake, most of us will take personal salvation over the empire of God any day. So we prefer our Christ crucified, a once living Jesus silenced by a higher calling.

But this was not so for the friends and followers of Jesus. For them, the empire of God *was* salvation. They saw God's care for them in the communities of mutual care and love founded in Jesus' name. They experienced the acceptance and welcome they received around the tables of the Jesus movement as redemption. Beggars, lepers, prostitutes, and expendables of every sort—the "nothings" of the world, as Paul puts it—embraced Jesus' empire of God as their one great hope and longing. Others did too—people like Paul, who gave up lives of considerable status and importance to enter into these communities of the new empire. Why did they do it? They were responding to the compelling vision of Jesus, who lived on for them, alive in their midst. For them, this was no existential metaphor for commitment. Jesus was really alive, spiritually present with them. Whatever it might mean to speak thus today about Jesus—to say that he is "alive" in our midst—it must above all else mean that he somehow still offers us the vision of a new empire, into which we are still invited in a very real way. Apart from his words and deeds, the living Jesus would have meant nothing to those who encountered him in the private and public places of antiquity. Neither can Jesus be alive to us apart from his words and deeds. He is alive to *us* only as he was alive to them, as a real invitation into a way of life we can see reflected in his own life, and the God to be encountered there.

Notes

Prologue: The Crucifixion of a Nobody

1. On the connection between Christian anti-Semitism and the way Christians have chosen to remember Jesus' death, see James Carroll's compelling account in *Constantine's Sword: The Church and the Jews—A History* (Boston: Houghton Mifflin, 2001).

2. For crucifixion as a Roman form of punishment see Paul Winter, *The Trial of Jesus*, 2d ed., rev. and ed. T. A. Burkill and Geza Vermes, SJ (Berlin: de Gruyter, 1974), 90–96; also Richard Horsley, "The Death of Jesus," in *Studying the Historical Jesus: Evaluations of the State of Current Research,* ed. Bruce Chilton and Craig Evans, NTTS 19 (Leiden: Brill, 1994), 409–13.

3. Josephus, *War* 2.66-75; *Ant.* 17.286-98.

4. Josephus, *War* 2.308-9.

5. This is Crossan's term in *Jesus: A Revolutionary Biography* (San Francisco: HarperSanFrancisco, 1994), 127.

6. For discussion see Ekkehard W. Stegemann and Wolfgang Stegemann, *The Jesus Movement: A Social History of Its First Century,* trans. O. C. Dean Jr. (Minneapolis: Fortress Press, 1999), 118.

7. Most scholars seem to agree that the Temple incident depicted in Mark 11:15-19 (also Matt 21:12-13 and Luke 19:45-46) and John 2:14-16 recalls an actual event that ultimately brought about Jesus' death; see, e.g., E. P. Sanders, *Jesus and Judaism* (Philadelphia: Fortress Press, 1985), 61–76; John Dominic Crossan, *The Historical Jesus: The Life of a Mediterranean Jewish Peasant* (San Francisco: HarperSanFrancisco, 1991), 355–60; Richard Horsley, *Jesus and the Spiral of Violence* (San Francisco: Harper & Row, 1987), 292–300; Marcus Borg, *Jesus, a New Vision: Spirit, Culture, and the Life of Discipleship* (San Francisco: Harper & Row, 1987), 174–76; but cf. Robert J. Miller, "Historical Method and the Deeds of Jesus: The Test Case of the Temple Destruction," *Forum* 8, nos. 1-2 (1992) 5–30, for a contrary view.

8. Crossan, *Jesus: A Revolutionary Biography*, 154.

Victim

1. Klaus Wengst's sobering treatment is most helpful: *Pax Romana and the Peace of Jesus Christ,* trans. John Bowden (Philadelphia: Fortress Press, 1987), 7–55.

2. The reference is to Augustus's *Res Gestae Divi Augustus*, an autobiographical account of his accomplishments written near the end of his life. A copy of the document was found inscribed in the temple of Rome and Augustus at Ancyra: *CIL* 3.769-99; for a translation, see Naphtali Lewis and Meyer Reinhold, *Roman Civilization,* 2 vols. (New York: Harper & Row, 1966), 2.9–19.

3. As recounted by Josephus in *Ant.* 17.288-95.

4. For ancient practices generally see Thomas F. Carney, *The Shape of the Past* (Lawrence, Kans.: Coronado, 1975); for Roman practices see Paul Veyne, "The Roman Empire (Where Public Life Was Private)," in *A History of Private Life*, vol. 1: *From Pagan Rome to Byzantium,* ed. Paul Veyne, trans. Arthur Goldhammer (Cambridge: Harvard Univ. Press, 1987), 95–115; also Peter Garnsey and Richard Saller, "Patronal Power Relations," in *Paul and Empire: Religion and Power in Roman Imperial Society,* ed. Richard Horsley (Harrisburg: Trinity, 1997), 96–103.

5. The older view that the imperial cult was simply political, and therefore superficial, is currently under revision following the work of, among others, S. R. F. Price, *Rituals and Power* (Cambridge: Cambridge Univ. Press, 1984).

6. *OGIS* no. 458; for discussion, see Lewis and Reinhold, *Roman Civilization,* 2.64.

7. This decree was passed in 27 B.C.E., but not accepted by Augustus until 8 B.C.E., just a year after the Asian province began celebrating his birthday as the New Year (see previous note). The decree is discussed in Macrobius, *Saturnalia* 1.12.35 (for text and discussion see Lewis and Reinhold, *Roman Civilization,* 2.65).

8. For a description and study of the ancient city see Kenneth G. Holum, et al., *King Herod's Dream—Caesarea on the Sea* (New York: Norton, 1988).

9. Note that the manuscript tradition is at odds over whether Jesus was remembered as a *tektōn*, or merely the son of a *tektōn*, a dispute that perhaps reflects the unseemly background all of this implies.

10. For this correction to earlier notions of Jesus coming from a "middle-class" background we are indebted to John Dominic Crossan, *Jesus: A Revolutionary Biography* (San Francisco: HarperSanFrancisco, 1994), 23–26, making use of the work of Gerhard Lenski on the structure of ancient agrarian societies in *Power and Privilege* (New York: McGraw-Hill, 1966). Crossan also

notes, following Ramsay MacMullen, that *tektōn* was a common term of derision in Roman times. See MacMullen, *Roman Social Relations: 50 B.C.–A.D. 384* (New Haven: Yale Univ. Press, 1974), 17–18, 107–8, 139–40, and 198 n. 82.

11. For the commercialization of agriculture and concentration of land in the hands of fewer and fewer large owners see Ekkehard W. Stegemann and Wolfgang Stegemann, *The Jesus Movement: A Social History of Its First Century*, trans. O. C. Dean Jr. (Minneapolis: Fortress Press, 1999), 104–13; for the tax/tribute situation in first century Palestine see 113–25. On commercialization under Herodian and later Roman rule see also John Dominic Crossan and Jonathan Reed, *Excavating Jesus: Beneath the Stones, Behind the Texts* (San Francisco: HarperSanFrancisco, 2001), 54–70.

12. Lenski, *Power and Privilege*, 281–84.

13. The use of the term "empire," rather than "kingdom" or "reign," may at first seem jarring, but this is what Greek *basileia* means in the Hellenistic world. The challenge to Rome's imperial vision implied by the provocative use of this term was intentional, in my view.

14. John Dominic Crossan, *The Historical Jesus: The Life of a Mediterranean Jewish Peasant* (San Francisco: HarperCollins, 1991), 332–48.

15. Cf. Richard Horsley, *Jesus and the Spiral of Violence* (San Francisco: Harper & Row, 1987), 309–10.

16. Marcel Detienne and Jean-Pierre Vernant, *Cunning Intelligence in Greek Culture and Society*, trans. Janet Lloyd (Atlantic Highlands, N.J.: Humanities, 1978).

17. Is the story historical? Quite possibly, though the arguments do not fall clearly one way or the other. It coheres with the charge brought against Jesus in Luke's version of the trial before Pilate: "We found this man perverting our nation, and forbidding us to give tribute to Caesar, and saying that he himself is Christ a king" (Luke 23:3). This was clearly an issue with the early followers of Jesus, and so probably with Jesus himself.

18. Marcus Borg, *Jesus, a New Vision: Spirit, Culture, and the Life of Discipleship* (San Francisco: Harper & Row, 1987), especially 23–75.

19. On the dim view of magic taken by Romans see Mary Beard, John North, and S. R. F. Price, *Religions of Rome* (Cambridge: Cambridge Univ. Press, 1998), 1.211–44; 2.260–87. By the beginning of the first century C.E., magic of all sorts was considered illegal under the "Cornelian law on murderers and poisoners," passed under Lucius Cornelius Sulla in 81–80 B.C.E., which remained in force at least until the late third, or early fourth century C.E., as shown by commentary on the law from Justinian (*Digest* 48.8.3), Paulus (*Opinions* 5.23.14-19), and its reiteration in the *Theodosian Code* 9.16.3; see Beard, North, and Price, *Religions of Rome*, 2.261–63. For further discus-

sion of magic and its perceived threat to the Roman Empire, see Ramsay MacMullen, *Enemies of the Roman Order: Treason, Unrest, and Alienation in the Empire* (Cambridge: Harvard Univ. Press, 1966), 97–127. That pagan opponents of Christianity regarded it as *supertitio*, and its adherents (including Jesus himself) as magicians, is well known from Justin Martyr (*First Apology* 30; *Dialogue with Trypho* 69.7) and Origen (*Against Celsus* 1.6, 28, 68; 4.33; 6.38-41; 8.37).

20. I. M. Lewis, *Ecstatic Religion: An Anthropological Study of Spirit Possession and Shamanism* (Baltimore: Penguin, 1971).

21. Crossan, *Jesus: A Revolutionary Biography*, 88–91.

22. Crossan, *Jesus: A Revolutionary Biography,* 91, citing Barrie Reynolds, *Magic, Divination and Witchcraft among the Barotse of Northern Rhodesia*, Robins Series 3 (Berkeley: Univ. of California Press, 1963), 133–38.

23. Ibid.

24. See, e.g., E. P. Sanders, *Jesus and Judaism* (Philadelphia: Fortress Press, 1985), 61–76; Crossan, *Historical Jesus*, 355–60; Horsley, *Jesus and the Spiral of Violence*, 292–300; Borg, *Jesus: The New Vision*, 174–76; but cf. Robert J. Miller, "Historical Method and the Deeds of Jesus: The Test Case of the Temple Destruction," *Forum* 8, nos. 1-2 (1992) 5–30, for a contrary view.

25. The inscription is to be found in *OGIS* 2.48–60 (no. 458, lines 30-62); the translation (alt.) is from Lewis and Reinhold, eds., *Roman Civilization*, 2.64–65.

26. Dieter Georgi, *Theocracy in Paul's Praxis and Theology* (Minneapolis: Fortress Press, 1991), 28. The connection is also well documented by Wengst, *Pax Romana*, 76–79; and Helmut Koester, "Imperial Ideology and Paul's Eschatology in 1 Thessalonians," in *Paul and Empire*, ed. Horsley, 161–62.

27. Georgi, *Theocracy*, 26; see also Koester's remarks in "Imperial Ideology," 158, 160.

28. See especially James Kallas, "Romans XIII.1-7: An Interpolation," *NTS* 11 (1964) 365–74; W. Munroe, *Authority in Paul and Peter: The Identification of a Pastoral Stratum in the Pauline Corpus and 1 Peter* (Cambridge: Cambridge Univ. Press, 1983), 16–19; and J. C. O'Neill, *Paul's Letter to the Romans,* PNTC (Harmondsworth: Penguin, 1975), 207–9.

29. On the thoroughly anti-imperial stance of the Apocalypse of John see most recently Steven J. Friesen, *Imperial Cults and the Apocalypse of John* (New York: Oxford Univ. Press, 2001).

30. Pliny, *Ep.* 10.96.

31. On the mix of piety, power, and politics that characterized the imperial cult see especially Price, *Rituals and Power*.

Martyr

1. For discussion, see Lawrence M. Wills, *The Jew in the Court of the Foreign King: Ancient Jewish Court Legends,* HDR 26 (Minneapolis: Fortress Press, 1990).

2. George W. E. Nickelsburg, *Resurrection, Immortality, and Eternal Life in Intertestamental Judaism,* HTS 26 (Cambridge: Harvard Univ. Press, 1972), especially 48–62.

3. For the relationship between the songs of Second Isaiah and the hymns of the Wisdom of Solomon 2 and 4–5, see ibid., 62–65.

4. The existence of a pre-Markan passion narrative is to be sure a fractious debate not to be settled here. For an informative if tendentious discussion, see Burton L. Mack, *A Myth of Innocence: Mark and Christian Origins* (Philadelphia: Fortress Press, 1988), 249–68. Mack notes well the troubling apologetic interests involved in the quest for a pre-Markan passion narrative as an historically reliable account of Jesus' final days. Yet Mack's conclusion, drawn from the work of Werner Kelber, et al., in *The Passion in Mark: Studies on Mark 14–16* (Philadelphia: Fortress Press, 1976), that Mark created the passion sequence on his own is unsatisfactory since it necessitates the dependence of the Gospel of John and the *Gospel of Peter* on Mark for the episodes they all share in common, something I find unlikely. Preferable, in my view, is the analysis of Helmut Koester, who argues instead that Mark, John, and the *Gospel of Peter* all rely on a common source (*Ancient Christian Gospels* [Philadelphia: Trinity Press International, 1990], 220–30). Consequently, I would continue to foster the theory of a pre-Markan passion narrative, but without the usual accompanying assumption of its basic historicity. The *fictional* work Mack and others ascribe to Mark must simply be moved back to a pre-Markan stage.

5. "The Genre and Function of the Markan Passion Narrative," *HTR* 73 (1980) 153–84. Nickelsburg's treatment is the most elegant, but his insights about the use of the tradition of the suffering righteous one were anticipated by several, including C. H. Dodd, *According to the Scriptures: The Sub-Structure of New Testament Theology* (New York: Scribner's, 1953); Barnabas Lindars, *New Testament Apologetic: The Doctrinal Significance of the Old Testament Quotations* (Philadelphia: Westminster, 1961); Eta Linnemann, *Studien zur Passionsgeschichte,* FRLANT 102 (Göttingen: Vandenhoeck & Ruprecht, 1970). Detlev Dormeyer's study, *Die Passion Jesu als Verhaltensmodell: Literarische und theologische Analyse der Traditions- und Redaktionsgeschichte der Markuspassion,* NTA 11 (Münster: Aschendorff, 1974), adds independent weight to the discussion.

6. Mack, *Myth of Innocence,* 267.

7. For a list of allusions in the passion narrative to the psalms of the righteous sufferer and the Servant Songs of Second Isaiah, see Joel Marcus, "The Role of Scripture in the Gospel Passion Narratives," in *The Death of Jesus in Early Christianity,* ed. John Carroll and Joel Green (Peabody, Mass.: Hendrickson, 1995), especially 207–9 and 214–15.

8. Among recent treatments of the Noble Death tradition and its significance for understanding the New Testament are David Seeley, *The Noble Death: Greco-Roman Martyrology and Paul's Concept of Salvation,* JSNTSup 28 (Sheffield: JSOT Press, 1990); and Arthur J. Droge and James D. Tabor, *A Noble Death: Suicide and Martyrdom among Christians and Jews in Antiquity* (San Francisco: HarperSanFrancisco, 1992). Earlier, see Martin Hengel, *The Atonement: The Origins of the Doctrine in the New Testament,* trans. John Bowden (Philadelphia: Fortress Press, 1981), 1–32.

9. Sam K. Williams, *Jesus' Death as Saving Event: The Background and Origin of a Concept,* HDR 2 (Missoula, Mont.: Scholars Press, 1975), 153–61.

10. Seeley, *Noble Death,* 13, 83, 87–99, *et passim.*

11. For the Antiochene provenance of Fourth Maccabees see especially André Dupont-Sommer, *Le Quatrième Livre des Machabées,* Bibliothèque de l'École des Hautes Études 274 (Paris: Librairie Ancienne Honré Champion, 1939), 69–73; Moses Hadas, *The Third and Fourth Books of Maccabees* (New York: Harper & Brothers, 1953), 109–13; and Williams, *Jesus' Death as Saving Event,* 248–53. This judgment seems persuasive to me, *pace* the judicious treatment of this still disputed matter by H. Anderson, "4 Maccabees: A New Translation and Introduction," in *OTP* 2.534–37.

12. Seeley's analysis of Fourth Maccabees is most helpful: *Noble Death,* 92–99. Seeley is not the first, however, to see the significance of the Maccabean literature for understanding the martyrological background of early Christian interpretation of Jesus' death. Eduard Lohse developed it in his study, *Märtyrer und Gottesknecht: Untersuchungen zur urchristlichen Verkündigung vom Sühntod Jesu Christi,* FRLANT 64 (Göttingen: Vandenhoeck & Ruprecht, 1963), especially 66–72. Williams's study, *Jesus' Death as Saving Event,* upon which Seeley builds, advanced the discussion by locating the martyrological ideas evidenced especially in 4 Maccabees within the Hellenistic intellectual tradition of sacrificing oneself for a cause; similarly, Marinus de Jonge, "Jesus' Death for Others and the Maccabean Martyrs," in *Text and Testimony: Festschrift for A. F. J. Klijn,* ed. T. Baarda, et al. (Kampen: Kok, 1988), 142–51.

13. The idea that the noble death could be "sacrificial" and atoning is significant for early Christian notions of Jesus' death as a sacrifice, and the subject of Williams's study, *Jesus' Death as Saving Event.* I will take up this important subject in the next chapter.

14. For Antioch as the home of both the Maccabean tradition and certain early Christian traditions, and the importance of this geographic coincidence in accounting for the emergence of these ideas in early Christianity, see Williams, *Jesus Death as Saving Event*, 233–54.

15. See David Seeley's helpful analysis in "The Background of the Philippians Hymn (2:6-11)," *Journal of Higher Criticism* 1 (1994) 49–72.

16. This is Seeley's insight; see *Noble Death*, 92–94, *et passim*.

17. For the Stoic parallels here see Victor Paul Furnish, *II Corinthians*, AB 32A (Garden City, N.Y.: Doubleday, 1984), 281.

18. Note the "caution required by the apostle's eschatology" (Ernst Käsemann, *Commentary on Romans*, trans. and ed. Geoffrey W. Bromiley [Grand Rapids: Eerdmans, 1980], 166).

19. That Paul must balance his indicatives here with imperatives underscores his realism about the continuing human situation—so Günther Bornkamm, "Baptism and New Life in Paul (Romans 6)," in *Early Christian Experience*, trans. Paul L. Hammer (New York: Harper & Row, 1969), 71–86.

20. The martyrological aspects of Mark are emphasized especially by Mack, *Myth of Innocence*, especially 320–21, 340–49.

21. Norman Perrin, *The New Testament: An Introduction* (New York: Harcourt, Brace, Jovanovich, 1974), 144–45; idem, "The Evangelist as Author," in *Parable and Gospel*, ed. K. C. Hanson, FCBS (Minneapolis: Fortress Press, 2003), 58.

22. The use of the term *paradidonai* may reflect the terminology of the Servant Songs of Second Isaiah (Isa 53:6, 12)—so Joel Marcus, *The Way of the Lord: Christological Exegesis of the Old Testament in the Gospel of Mark* (Louisville: Westminster John Knox, 1992), 188–89. That the Servant Songs could take on collective significance in Jewish exegesis of Isaiah (Marcus, *Way of the Lord*, 190–93) perhaps offers Mark the poetic license to identify John, Jesus, and anyone who would follow them with Isaiah's suffering righteous servant.

23. See 1 Cor 11:23-25.

24. Isa 53:12 (MT).

25. The martyrological aspects of the Last Supper in Mark are brought out especially by Dennis Smith in *From Symposium to Eucharist: The Banquet in the Early Christian World* (Minneapolis: Fortress Press, 2003), 247–53.

26. On the Johannine situation and the question of martyrdom see the benchmark study by J. Louis Martyn, *History and Theology in the Fourth Gospel*, rev. ed. (Nashville: Abingdon, 1979); also, idem, *The Gospel of John in Christian History: Essays for Interpreters*, Theological Inquiries (New York: Paulist, 1978), 90–121. One should bear in mind, however, that there is no evidence of widespread persecution of Christians by Jews in this or later periods. John's

experience is a local experience, and we know it only through his perception and presentation of it.

27. The complexity of themes and issues in John serves often to obscure what otherwise might be quite obvious. The martyrological aspects of John are seldom commented upon, though a notable exception is Paul Minear's subtle treatment in *John: The Martyr's Gospel* (New York: Pilgrim, 1984).

28. Wilhelm Bousset, *Kyrios Christos: A History of the Belief in Christ from the Beginnings of Christianity to Irenaeus,* trans. John E. Steely (Nashville: Abingdon, 1970) 217.

29. *The Martyrdom of Saints Perpetua and Felicitas*; for the text in translation see Herbert Musurillo, *The Acts of the Christian Martyrs* (Oxford: Oxford Univ. Press, 1972), 106-31.

30. *Perpetua and Felicitas* 21.

31. Hengel, *Atonement*, 14-15.

32. *Ep.* 24.11.

33. For the martyrological sense of the passage, particularly of the quotation from Ps 43:23, see Käsemann, *Romans*, 245-52, especially 249-50.

Sacrifice

1. Anthropology has not passed on the opportunity to fill in this lacuna of meaning; the theories are as impressive as they are imaginative. See William Robertson Smith, *The Religion of the Semites* (1889; reprint, New York: Schocken, 1972); Emile Durkheim, *The Elementary Forms of Religious Life,* trans. Joseph W. Swain (New York: Macmillan, 1915); Henri Hubert and Marcel Mauss, *Sacrifice: Its Nature and Function,* trans. W. D. Halls (Chicago: Univ. of Chicago Press, 1964); Walter Burkert, *Homo Necans,* trans. Peter Bing (Berkeley: Univ. of California Press, 1983); René Girard, *Violence and the Sacred,* trans. Patrick Gregory (Baltimore: Johns Hopkins Univ. Press, 1977).

2. *Theogony* 535ff.

3. For this insight, and the approach that follows from it, see the collection of essays from colleagues at the Center for Comparative Research on Ancient Societies edited by Marcel Detienne and Jean-Pierre Vernant, *The Cuisine of Sacrifice among the Greeks,* trans. Paula Wissing (Chicago: Univ. of Chicago Press, 1989).

4. Marcel Detienne, "Culinary Practices and the Spirit of Sacrifice," in ibid., 11. Only the meat of smaller animals, like chickens or fish (usually), was not sacrificed.

5. Jean-Pierre Vernant, "At Man's Table: Hesiod's Foundation Myth of Sacrifice," in *Cuisine of Sacrifice*, 25–26, citing Jean Casabona, *Reserches sur le vocabulaire des sacrifices en grec, des origins à la fin de l'époque classique* (Aix-en-Provence: Ophrys, 1966). *Hierō* can mean either "to slaughter" or "to sacrifice" in Homeric and Classical usage. Later the term *thyō* can mean "to sacrifice," "to feast," or "to slaughter" (LSJ, s.v. *thyō*). For the unity of sacrifice and feasting, see Dennis E. Smith, *From Symposium to Eucharist: The Banquet in the Early Christian World* (Minneapolis: Fortress Press, 2003), 67–69.

6. Detienne, "Culinary Practices," 11.

7. This basic description of a Greek sacrifice comes from Burkert, *Homo Necans*, 3–7, with assembled details from Homer and the Greek tragedians. Helpful details and insights are also to be found in Jean-Louis Durand's essay, "Greek Animals: Toward a Typology of Edible Bodies," in *The Cuisine of Sacrifice among the Greeks,* edited by Marcel Detienne and Jean-Pierre Vernant, 87–118 (Chicago: Univ. of Chicago Press, 1989).

8. Note this critique from Stanley K. Stowers, "Greeks Who Sacrifice and Those Who Do Not," in *The Social World of the First Christians: Essays in Honor of Wayne A. Meeks,* ed. L. Michael White and O. Larry Yarbrough (Minneapolis: Fortress Press, 1995), 297–98.

9. Detienne, "Culinary Practices," 13. Plato speaks of the *geras*, or "meat privilege" (*Phaedrus* 265e; *Politicus* 287c), whereby the choice pieces of the animal are given first to the dignitaries present, but the more ancient practice seems to have been strictly egalitarian, with equal portions of meat distributed to all by lottery.

10. See especially the discussion by Stowers, "Greeks Who Sacrifice," 323–29. Stowers's perspective is a corrective to those who have tended to view Hellenistic sacrificial practice in terms of the Homeric ideal of citizens sharing equally in the distribution of the sacrificial meat. Yet, even before the changes brought on by the early imperial period, the distribution of meat portions was not strictly egalitarian, with multiple and choice portions going to city and cult officials before the common portions were distributed to the gathered crowd. A late-fourth-century Attic inscription lists the following recipients and their allotted shares: "Five pieces each to the presidents / Five pieces each to the nine archons / One piece each to the treasurers of the goddess / One piece each to the managers of the feast / The customary portions to others" (*SIG* 271; as cited by Royden Keith Yerkes, *Sacrifice in Greek and Roman Religions and Early Judaism* [New York: Scribner's, 1952], 107–8).

11. For the principle, and its notable exceptions, see Detienne, "The Violence of Wellborn Ladies: Women in the Thesmophoria," in *Cuisine of Sacrifice,* ed. Detienne and Vernant, 129–47.

12. Durand, "Greek Animals," 104.

13. See Mary Beard, John North, and Simon Price, *Religions of Rome*, vol. 1: *A History* (Cambridge: Cambridge Univ. Press, 1998), 37–38, for a discussion of the phenomenon; and vol. 2: *A Sourcebook*, 172–74, for examples.

14. Pliny, *Natural History* 10.33 (LCL).

15. For discussion see Martin Hengel, *The Atonement: The Origins of the Doctrine in the New Testament*, trans. John Bowden (Philadelphia: Fortress Press, 1981), 24–28; and Adela Yarbro Collins, "Finding Meaning in the Death of Jesus," *HR* 78 (1998) 185–87.

16. See Hengel, *Atonement*, 19, n. 65.

17. See Hengel, *Atonement*, 19–24, for discussion and the examples that follow.

18. Lycurgus, *Oratio in Leocratium* 24.

19. Pausanius, *Description of Greece* 9.17.1.

20. For the father, see Livy, *Roman History* 8.9; for the son, see Livy, *Roman History* 10.28; for grandson, see Plutarch, *Pyrrhus* 21; and Dionysus of Halicarnassus, *Roman Antiquities* 20.1.

21. *Roman History* 10.28 (LCL).

22. *Civil War* 2.314-15 (LCL).

23. *Civil War* 2.305 (LCL).

24. H. Anderson, trans., in *OTP* 2, 552.

25. This basic understanding of how the sprinkling of sacrificial blood works as a cleansing agent, not of the sinner, but of the cultic sanctuary, is the insight of Jacob Milgrom, "Israel's Sanctuary: The Priestly 'Picture of Dorian Gray,'" *RB* 83 (1976) 390–99; reprinted in idem, *Studies in Cultic Theology and Terminology*, SJLA 36 (Leiden: Brill, 1983), 75–84.

26. *Purity and Danger: An Analysis of the Concepts of Pollution and Taboo* (London: Routledge and Kegan Paul, 1966), 35.

27. For a discussion, see Wendy Cotter, "The Collegia and Roman Law: State Restrictions on Voluntary Associations, 64 B.C.E.–200 C.E.," in *Voluntary Associations in the Graeco-Roman World*, ed. John S. Kloppenborg and Stephen G. Wilson (London: Routledge, 1996), 74–89.

28. On the significance of meals in the early Jesus movement see Burton L. Mack, *A Myth of Innocence: Mark and Christian Origins* (Minneapolis: Fortress Press, 1988), 80–83; Hal Taussig and Dennis E. Smith, *Many Tables: The Eucharist in the New Testament* (Philadelphia: Trinity, 1990), 48–50; and Dennis Smith, *From Symposium to Eucharist*, 173–80, especially on meals in the Pauline tradition.

29. That early followers of Jesus came to understand his death as sacrificial primarily through the Jewish and broader Hellenistic martyrological tra-

dition is argued most impressively by Sam K. Williams, *Jesus' Death as Saving Event: The Background and Origin of a Concept*, HDR 2 (Missoula, Mont.: Scholars Press, 1975). See also the remarks of Rowan Williams, *Eucharistic Sacrifice: The Roots of a Metaphor* (Bramcote: Grove, 1982), 13–15.

30. The point is pressed by David Seeley, *The Noble Death: Greco-Roman Martyrology and Paul's Concept of Salvation*, JSNTSup 28 (Sheffield: JSOT Press, 1990), especially 87–94.

31. See Richard B. Hays, *The Faith of Jesus Christ: An Investigation of the Narrative Substructure of Galatians 3:1—4:11*, SBLDS 56 (Chico, Calif.: Scholars Press, 1983), 170–74, for discussion and literature.

32. Note that for Paul, in Romans, Jesus is designated Son of God by his resurrection (Rom 1:4).

33. So Hays, *Faith of Jesus Christ*, 173; see also his n. 135, commenting on the thesis of Goodenough (see n. 34 below).

34. This is closer to the approach taken by E. R. Goodenough in Goodenough and A. T. Kraabel, "Paul and the Hellenization of Christianity," in *Religions in Antiquity: Essays in Honor of Erwin Ramsdell Goodenough*, ed. Jacob Neusner, SHR 14 (Leiden: Brill, 1968), 45.

35. Smith, *From Sympoium to Eucharist*, 188–91.

36. Mack, *Myth of Innocence*, 216–19, 222–24; also Reginald H. Fuller, *The Foundations of New Testament Christology* (New York: Scribner's, 1965), 171; and Ferdinand Hahn, *The Titles of Jesus in Christology: Their History in Early Christianity*, trans. Harold Knight and George Ogg, Lutterworth Library (London: Lutterworth, 1969), 379.

37. Stowers, "Greeks Who Sacrifice," 328.

38. Beard, North, and Price, *Religions of Rome*, 1.361.

39. Similarly Williams, *Eucharistic Sacrifice*, 6. Williams, however, stresses the efforts of later Christian apologists, like Justin Martyr, to overcome the charge of subversion by depicting the Eucharist as a sacrifice that ought to be seen as a "normal and acceptable traditional form of piety" (8). But one should probably understand Justin to be putting the best possible spin on a practice that was conceived and perceived as subversive to the state.

40. Gerd Theissen, "The Strong and the Weak in Corinth," in *The Social Setting of Pauline Christianity: Essays on Corinth*, trans. John H. Schütz (Philadelphia: Fortress Press, 1982), 126.

41. See the succinct summary by Theissen in ibid., 127–28; or the more recent and all-inclusive survey by Dennis Smith in *From Symposium to Eucharist*, 13–172.

42. "The Strong and the Weak," 125–32.

43. Alan F. Segal, *Paul the Convert: The Apostolate and Apostasy of Saul the Pharisee* (New Haven: Yale Univ. Press, 1990), 231–32.

44. For *synedeisis* as "consciousness," not "conscience," see Richard A. Horsley, "Consciousness and Freedom among the Corinthians: 1 Cor 8–10," *CBQ* 40 (1978) 581–85.

45. David Gill, "*Trapezomata*: A Neglected Aspect of Greek Sacrifice," *HTR* 67 (1974) 123–27.

46. Cf. Richard A. Horsley's excellent treatment of this issue in 1 Corinthians in "1 Corinthians: A Case Study of Paul's Assembly as an Alternative Society," in *Paul and Empire: Religion and Power in Roman Imperial Society,* ed. Richard A. Horsley (Harrisburg: Trinity, 1997), 242–52, esp. 247–49.

47. There is little evidence that Christians suffered general persecution during this time frame. Nonetheless, we should probably assume that they suffered to the same extent that all dissidents to the empire suffered, and more severely in some places than in others; see Frederick J. Murphy, *Fallen Is Babylon: The Revelation to John,* New Testament in Context (Harrisburg: Trinity, 1998), 5–17.

48. Ludwig Mitteis and Ulrich Wilcken, *Grundzüge und Chrestomathie der Papyruskunde,* I, 2 (Leipzig: Teubner, 1912), no. 124, as cited and translated in Beard, North, and Price, *Religions of Rome,* 2.165.

49. Beard, North, and Price, *Religions of Rome,* 1.239. Note, however, that in places where the Roman cultus was particularly established and prominent, the Christian affront was understood to be directed more specifically to Roman religious customs (so Beard, North, and Price, *Religions of Rome,* 1.239–41).

50. Jonathan Z. Smith, *Map Is Not Territory: Studies in the History of Religions,* SJLA 23 (Chicago: Univ. of Chicago Press, 1993), xi–xv and 67–207, passim; and idem, *Drudgery Divine: On the Comparison of Early Christianities and the Religions of Late Antiquity* (Chicago: Univ. of Chicago Press, 1990), 121–25.

51. Smith, *Map Is Not Territory,* 138.

52. On the various techniques for interpreting Scripture in Hebrews see Harold W. Attridge's succinct summary in *The Epistle to the Hebrews,* Hermeneia (Philadelphia: Fortress Press, 1989), 23–25.

53. Passages such as 7:11-19, often used to make this case, are not anti-Jewish. Rather, the author typically critiques aspects of Jewish (cultic) tradition by making use of other Jewish traditions.

54. 3:6; 10:19; 10:35.

55. 10:36; 12:2; 12:7.

56. 3:6; 6:11.

57. Especially 11:1-40; see below.

58. Ernst Käsemann, *The Wandering People of God: An Investigation of the Letter to the Hebrews,* trans. Roy A. Harrisville and Irving L. Sandberg (Minneapolis: Augsburg, 1984), 174–82.

59. Attridge (*Epistle to the Hebrews,* 22): "fidelity [in chap. 11] encompasses both the more static virtue of endurance, exemplified particularly in Israel's martyrs (11:35-38) and in some aspects the story of Moses (11:25, 27), but also the 'dynamic' virtue of movement. In the exemplars of faith, this movement is not entry but exit."

The Resurrection of a Nobody

1. Rodolfo Lanciani, *Ancient Rome in the Light of Recent Discoveries* (Boston: Houghton Mifflin, 1888), 122.

2. *Against Heresies* 2.32.4.

3. The matter of what the Corinthians actually believed is disputed. The view expressed here is held by a number of scholars, including Ulrich Wilckens, *Weisheit und Torheit* (Tübingen: Mohr/Siebeck, 1959), 11; Ernst Käsemann, *New Testament Questions of Today,* trans. W. I. Montague (Philadelphia: Fortress Press, 1969), 125–26; J. H. Wilson, "The Corinthians Who Say There Is No Resurrection," *ZNW* 59 (1968) 90–107; James M. Robinson, "Kerygma and History in the New Testament," in idem and Helmut Koester, *Trajectories Through Early Christianity* (Philadelphia: Fortress Press, 1971), 33–34; and Jürgen Becker, *Auferstehung der Toten im Urchristentum,* SBS 82 (Stuttgart: Katholisches Bibelwerk, 1976), 74–76; although see E. Earle Ellis for a skeptical assessment: "Christ Crucified," in *Reconciliation and Hope,* ed. Robert Banks (Grand Rapids: Eerdmans, 1974), 73–74.

4. That such a view developed among the followers of Paul is shown by 2 Tim 2:17-18, which attributes it to a certain Hymenaeus (also mentioned as an opponent of the Pastor in 1 Tim 1:20) and Phyletus.

5. The question of how to understand surrogate baptism in this text is also a thorny problem. Most scholars take the plain sense of the text to be that people in Corinth were being baptized vicariously on behalf of dead relatives or friends. See, e.g., Hans Lietzmann, *An die Korinther I-II,* HNT 9 (Tübingen: Mohr/Siebeck, 1949), 82; Hans Conzelmann, *1 Corinthians: A Commnetary,* trans. James W. Leitch, Hermeneia (Philadelphia: Fortress Press, 1975), 275; and Andreas Lindemann, *Der Erste Korintherbrief,* HNT 9/1 (Tübingen: Mohr/Siebeck, 2000), 350–51.

6. Robert Martin-Achard, "Resurrection: Old Testament," *ABD* 5.683: "We draw attention to the fact that the theme of the resurrection asserted itself in

the Jewish milieu at the very moment when apocalyptic views were developing in answer to the distress being undergone by faithful Jews. By the victory over death . . . justice was rendered to the Yahwistic faithful."

7. One of the great themes of Jewish and Hellenistic martyrological literature is the overcoming of physical vulnerability; see David Seeley, *The Noble Death: Greco-Roman Martyrology and Paul's Concept of Salvation,* JSNTSup 28 (Sheffield: JSOT Press 1990), 96–97, 118–24, 126–27, 128–29, 131–32.

8. The importance of this simple point, seldom emphasized, is seen especially by Ulrich Wilckens, *Resurrection: Biblical Testimony to the Resurrection—An Historical Examination and Explanation,* trans. A. M. Stewart (Atlanta: John Knox, 1978), 124–32.

9. Most recently, e.g., N. T. Wright, *The Resurrection of the Son of God* (Minneapolis: Fortress Press, 2003), 696: "the combination of empty tomb and appearances of the living Jesus forms a set of circumstances which is itself *both necessary and sufficient* for the rise of early Christian belief. Without these phenomena, we cannot explain why this belief came into existence, and took the shape it did." Others have doubted it, however. See especially Rudolf Pesch, "Zur Entstehung des Glaubens an die Auferstehung Jesu," *ThQ* 153 (1973) 201–28, who argues that postresurrection visionary experiences and the like "did not occasion the origin of Easter faith, but confirmed this faith" (152). So also most notably Edward Schillebeeckx, *Jesus: An Experiment in Christology,* trans. Hubert Hoskins (New York: Seabury, 1979), especially 379–97. Though Schillebeeckx does allow that the disciples scattered after Jesus' crucifixion, he does not postulate the resurrection as that seminal "event" that brought them back together. Their "conversion" from fear involved foremost the "remembered aspects of their life shared in fellowship with Jesus and of Jesus' whole line of conduct." Though they had failed, they "had not in the end lost their faith in Jesus" (382).

10. Scholars have been slow in persuading translators to abandon the traditional rendering of this verse using the word "to" rather than "in," even though most translations now note that Paul does not really say "to me" in the Greek of this verse, but "in me" (*en emoi*).

11. The Greek word *pneuma* has many meanings: spirit, wind, breath, and ghost.

12. Hans Dieter Betz, "Zum Problem der Auferstehung Jesus im Lichte der griechischen magischen Papyri," in *Hellenismus und Urchristentum: Gesammelte Aufsätze,* vol. 1 (Tübingen: Mohr/Siebeck, 1990), 230–61, especially 254–58.

13. As first proposed by Julius Wellhausen, *Das Evangelium Marci* (Berlin: Reimer, 1909), 71. The mountaintop setting, the luminous appearance of Jesus and his companions, Moses and Elijah, and the idea in popular Jewish

lore that these latter two figures had been translated to heaven, are generally regarded as evidence that the story was originally a postresurrection appearance story. Jesus has now joined the company of those whose fate was finally to dwell with God in heaven. Mark easily transforms it into a story designed to predict Jesus' fate.

14. Rudolf Bultmann, *Die Geschichte der synoptischen Tradition, Ergänzungsheft*, 81; more recently, John Dominic Crossan, *The Historical Jesus: The Life of a Mediterranean Jewish Peasant* (San Francisco: HarperSanFrancisco, 1991), 405.

15. Adela Yarbro Collins, *The Beginning of the Gospel: Probings of Mark in Context* (Minneapolis: Fortress Press, 1992), 138–43.

16. The formula exists in three basic forms: (1) a participial construction describing God as "the one who raised him [Jesus] from the dead" (Rom 4:24; 8:11a, b; 2 Cor 4:14; Gal 1:1); (2) a simple finite construction: "God raised him [Jesus] from the dead" (Rom 10:9; 1 Cor 6:14; 15:15); and (3) a relative construction modifying Jesus as the one "whom he [God] raised from the dead" (1 Thess 1:10). See Paul Hoffmann, "Auferstehung Jesu Christi: II/1. Neues Testament," in *TRE* 1.479–80.

17. So Hoffmann, "Auferstehung," 486.

18. For the martyrological overtones of Phil 2:8 see Seeley, *Noble Death*, 103.

19. That the contest over apostolic authority shaped the early Christian resurrection proclamation is clear. See Hans von Campenhausen, *Ecclesiastical Authority and Spiritual Power in the Church of the First Three Centuries* (Stanford: Stanford Univ. Press, 1969), 13–23; Pheme Perkins, *Resurrection: New Testament Witness and Contemporary Reflection* (Garden City, N.Y.: Doubleday, 1984), 193–214; Crossan, *Historical Jesus*, 395–416.

20. Marcus J. Borg, *Jesus, a New Vision: Spirit, Culture, and the Life of Discipleship* (San Francisco: Harper & Row, 1987), 23–75.

21. For a fascinating treatment, see Stevan L. Davies, *Jesus the Healer: Possession, Trance, and the Origins of Christianity* (New York: Continuum, 1995).

22. The Spirit: Rom 7:4; 8:4-6, 13, 16, 23, 26-27; 1 Cor 2:10; 12:4, 7-11, 13; 14:2; 2 Cor 1:22; 3:6, 8; 5:5; Gal 3:2-5, 14; 5:5, 18, 22, 25; 6:8; Phil 2:1; 1 Thess 5:19; God's Spirit: Rom 8:9, 14; 1 Cor 2:11, 14; 3:16; 6:11; 7:40; 12:3; 2 Cor 3:3; Phil 3:3; the Holy Spirit: Rom 5:5; 9:1; 14:7; 15:13, 16, 19; 1 Cor 6:19; 12:3; 2 Cor 6:6; 13:14; 1 Thess 1:5-6; 4:8; the Spirit of Life: Rom 8:2; the Spirit of the Lord: 2 Cor 3:17; the Spirit of Christ: Rom 9:2; or Jesus Christ: Phil 1:19; cf. the Spirit of his Son: Gal 4:6.

23. On this point see especially Willi Marxsen, "When Did Christian Faith Begin?" in *Jesus and the Church: The Beginnings of Christianity*, trans. and ed. Philip Devenish (Philadelphia: Trinity, 1992), 76–95.

Bibliography

Anderson, H. "4 Maccabees: A New Translation and Introduction." In *OTP* 2.531–64.

Attridge, Harold W. *The Epistle to the Hebrews*. Hermeneia. Philadelphia: Fortress Press, 1989.

Beard, Mary, John North, and Simon Price. *Religions of Rome*. Vol. 1: *A History*. Vol. 2: *A Sourcebook*. Cambridge: Cambridge Univ. Press, 1998.

Becker, Jürgen. *Auferstehung der Toten im Urchristentum*. SBS 82. Stuttgart: Katholisches Bibelwerk, 1976.

Betz, Hans Dieter. "Zum Problem der Auferstehung Jesus im Lichte der griechischen magischen Papyri." In *Hellenismus und Urchristentum: Gesammelte Aufsätze*, 1.230–61. 3 vols. Tübingen: Mohr/ Siebeck, 1990.

Borg, Marcus J. *Jesus, a New Vision: Spirit, Culture, and the Life of Discipleship*. San Francisco: Harper & Row, 1987.

Bornkamm, Günther. "Baptism and New Life in Paul (Romans 6)." In *Early Christian Experience*, 71–86. New York: Harper & Row, 1969.

Bousset, Wilhelm. *Kyrios Christos: A History of the Belief in Christ from the Beginnings of Christianity to Irenaeus*, trans. John E. Steely (Nashville: Abingdon, 1970).

Breytenbach, Cilliers. "'Christus starb für uns': Zur Tradition und paulinischen Rezeption der 'Sterbformel.'" *NTS* 49 (2003) 447–75.

Bultmann, Rudolf. *Die Geschichte der synoptischen Tradition, Ergänzungsheft*. Edited by Philipp Vielhauer and Gerd Theissen. 5th ed. FRLANT 29. Göttingen: Vandenhoeck & Ruprecht, 1979.

Burkert, Walter. *Homo Necans: The Anthropology of Ancient Greek Sacrificial Ritual and Myth*. Translated by Peter Bing. Berkeley: Univ. of California Press, 1983.

Campenhausen, Hans von. *Ecclesiastical Authority and Spiritual Power in the Church of the First Three Centuries*. Translated by J. A. Baker. Stanford: Stanford Univ. Press, 1969.

Carney, Thomas F. *The Shape of the Past: Models and Antiquity*. Lawrence, Kan.: Coronado, 1975.

Carroll, James. *Constantine's Sword: The Church and the Jews—A History*. Boston: Houghton Mifflin, 2001.

Casabona, Jean. *Reserches sur le vocabulaire des sacrifices en grec, des origins à la fin de l'époque classique*. Aix-en-Provence: Ophrys, 1966.

Charlesworth, James H., ed. *The Old Testament Pseudepigrapha*. 2 vols. Garden City, N.Y.: Doubleday, 1983–1985.

Collins, Adela Yarbro. *The Beginning of the Gospel: Probings of Mark in Context*. Minneapolis: Fortress Press, 1992.

———. "Finding Meaning in the Death of Jesus." *HR* 78 (1998) 175–96.

Conzelmann, Hans. *1 Corinthians: A Commentary*. Translated by James W. Leitch. Hermeneia. Philadelphia: Fortress Press, 1975.

Cotter, Wendy. "The Collegia and Roman Law: State Restrictions on Voluntary Associations, 64 B.C.E.–200 C.E." In *Voluntary Associations in the Graeco-Roman World*, edited by John S. Kloppenborg and Stephen G. Wilson, 74–89. London: Routledge, 1996.

Crossan, John Dominic. *The Historical Jesus: The Life of a Mediterranean Jewish Peasant*. San Francisco: HarperSanFrancisco, 1991.

———. *Jesus: A Revolutionary Biography*. San Francisco: HaperSanFrancisco, 1994.

———, and Jonathan L. Reed. *Excavating Jesus: Beneath the Stones, Behind the Texts*. San Francisco: HarperSanFrancisco, 2001.

Davies, Stevan L. *Jesus the Healer: Possession, Trance, and the Origins of Christianity*. New York: Continuum, 1995.

de Jonge, Marinus. "Jesus' Death for Others and the Maccabean Martyrs." In *Text and Testimony: Festschrift for A. F. J. Klijn*, edited by T. Baarda, et al., 142–51. Kampen: Kok, 1988.

Detienne, Marcel. "Culinary Practices and the Spirit of Sacrifice." In *The Cuisine of Sacrifice among the Greeks*, edited by M. Detienne and J.-P. Vernant, 1–20. Translated by Paula Wissing. Chicago: Univ. of Chicago Press, 1989.

———. "The Violence of Wellborn Ladies: Women in the Thesmophoria." In *The Cuisine of Sacrifice among the Greeks*, edited by M. Detienne and J.-P. Vernant, 129–47. Translated by Paula Wissing. Chicago: Univ. of Chicago Press, 1989.

———, and Jean-Pierre Vernant. *Cunning Intelligence in Greek Culture and Society*. Translated by Janet Lloyd. Atlantic Highlands, N.J.: Humanities, 1978.

———, eds. *The Cuisine of Sacrifice among the Greeks*. Translated by Paula Wissing. Chicago: Univ. of Chicago Press, 1989.

Dodd, C. H. *According to the Scriptures: The Sub-Structure of New Testament Theology*. New York: Scribner's, 1953.

Dormeyer, Detlev. *Die Passion Jesu als Verhaltensmodell: Literarische und theologische Analyse der Traditions- und Redaktionsgeschichte der Markuspassion.* NTA 11. Münster: Aschendorff, 1974.

Douglas, Mary. *Purity and Danger: An Analysis of the Concepts of Pollution and Taboo.* London: Routledge and Kegan Paul, 1966.

Droge, Arthur J., and James D. Tabor. *A Noble Death: Suicide and Martyrdom among Christians and Jews in Antiquity.* San Francisco: HarperSanFrancisco, 1992.

Dupont-Sommer, André. *Le Quatrième Livre des Machabées.* Bibliothèque de l'École des Hautes Études 274. Paris: Librairie Ancienne Honré Champion, 1939.

Durand, Jean-Louis. "Greek Animals: Toward a Typology of Edible Bodies." In *The Cuisine of Sacrifice among the Greeks,* edited by Marcel Detienne and Jean-Pierre Vernant, 87–118. Translated by Paula Wissing. Chicago: Univ. of Chicago Press, 1989.

Durkheim, Emil. *The Elementary Forms of Religious Life.* Translated by Joseph W. Swain. New York: Macmillan, 1915.

Ellis, E. Earle. "Christ Crucified." In *Reconciliation and Hope: New Testament Essays on Atonement and Eschatology Presented to L. L. Morris on His 60th Birthday,* edited by Robert Banks, 70–75. Grand Rapids: Eerdmans, 1974.

Friesen, Steven J. *Imperial Cults and the Apocalypse of John: Reading Revelation in the Ruins.* Oxford: Oxford Univ. Press, 2001.

Fuller, Reginald H. *The Foundations of New Testament Christology.* New York: Scribner's, 1965.

Furnish, Victor Paul. *II Corinthians.* AB 32A. Garden City, N.Y.: Doubleday, 1984.

Garnsey, Peter, and Richard P. Saller. "Patronal Power Relations." In *Paul and Empire: Religion and Power in Roman Imperial Society,* edited by Richard A. Horsley, 96–103. Harrisburg: Trinity, 1997.

Georgi, Dieter. *Theocracy in Paul's Praxis and Theology.* Translated by David E. Green. Minneapolis: Fortress Press, 1991.

Gill, David. "*Trapezomata*: A Neglected Aspect of Greek Sacrifice." *HTR* 67 (1974) 123–27.

Girard, René. *Violence and the Sacred.* Translated by Patrick Gregory. Baltimore: Johns Hopkins Univ. Press, 1977.

Goodenough, E. R., and Thomas A. Kraabel. "Paul and the Hellenization of Christianity." In *Religions in Antiquity: Eassays in Memory of Erwin Ramsdell Goodenough,* edited by Jacob Neusner, 35–80. SHR 14. Leiden: Brill, 1968.

Hadas, Moses. *The Third and Fourth Books of Maccabees.* New York: Harper, 1953.

Hahn, Ferdinand. *The Titles of Jesus in Christology: Their History in Early Christianity*. Translated by Harold Knight and George Ogg. Lutterworth Library. London: Lutterworth, 1969.

Hays, Richard B. *The Faith of Jesus Christ: An Investigation of the Narrative Substructure of Galatians 3:1—4:11*. SBLDS 56. Chico, Calif.: Scholars Press, 1983.

Hengel, Martin. *The Atonement: The Origins of the Doctrine in the New Testament*. Translated by John Bowden. Philadelphia: Fortress Press, 1981.

Hoffmann, Paul. "Auferstehung Jesu Christi: II/1. Neues Testament." *TRE* 1.479–80.

———. *Die Toten in Christus: Eine religionsgeschichtliche und exegetische Untersuchung zur paulinischen Eschatologie*. NTA 2. Münster: Aschendorf, 1966.

Holum, Kenneth G., et al. *King Herod's Dream—Caesarea on the Sea*. New York: Norton, 1988.

Horsley, Richard A. "1 Corinthians: A Case Study of Paul's Assembly as an Alternative Society." In *Paul and Empire: Religion and Power in Roman Imperial Society*, edited by Richard A. Horsley, 242–52. Harrisburg: Trinity, 1997.

———. "Consciousness and Freedom among the Corinthians: 1 Cor 8–10." *CBQ* 40 (1978) 581–85.

———. "The Death of Jesus." In *Studying the Historical Jesus: Evaluations of the State of Current Research*, edited by Bruce Chilton and Craig Evans, 395–422. NTTS 19. Leiden: Brill, 1994.

———. *Jesus and the Spiral of Violence: Popular Jewish Resistance in Roman Palestine*. San Francisco: Harper & Row, 1987.

Hubert, Henri, and Marcel Mauss. *Sacrifice: Its Nature and Function*. Translated by W. D. Halls. Chicago: Univ. of Chicago Press, 1964.

Käsemann, Ernst. *Commentary on Romans*. Translated and edited by Geoffrey W. Bromiley. Grand Rapids: Eerdmans, 1980.

———. *New Testament Questions of Today*. Translated by W. I. Montague. Philadelphia: Fortress Press, 1969.

———. *The Wandering People of God: An Investigation of the Letter to the Hebrews*. Translated by Roy Harrisville and Irvine L. Sandberg. Minneapolis: Augsburg, 1984.

Kallas, James. "Romans XIII.1-7: An Interpolation." *NTS* 11 (1964) 365–74.

Kelber, Werner, ed. *The Passion in Mark: Studies on Mark 14–16*. Philadelphia: Fortress Press, 1976.

Koester, Helmut. *Ancient Christian Gospels: Their History and Development*. Philadelphia: Trinity, 1990.

———. "Imperial Ideology and Paul's Eschatology in 1 Thessalonians." In *Paul and Empire: Religion and Power in Roman Imperial Society,* edited by Richard A. Horsley, 158–66. Harrisburg: Trinity, 1997.

———. "Jesus the Victim." *JBL* 111 (1992) 3–15.

Lenski, Gerhard E. *Power and Privilege: A Theory of Social Stratification.* New York: McGraw-Hill, 1966.

Lewis, I. M. *Ecstatic Religion: An Anthropological Study of Spirit Possession and Shamanism.* Baltimore: Penguin, 1971.

Lewis, Naphtali, and Meyer Reinhold. *Roman Civilization: Selected Readings.* 2 vols. New York: Harper & Row, 1966.

Lietzmann, Hans. *An die Korinther I-II.* HNT 9. Tübingen: Mohr/Siebeck, 1949.

Lindars, Barnabas. *New Testament Apologetic: The Doctrinal Significance of the Old Testament Quotations.* Philadelphia: Westminster, 1961.

Lindemann, Andreas. *Der Erste Korintherbrief.* HNT 9/1. Tübingen: Mohr/Siebeck, 2000.

Linnemann, Eta. *Studien zur Passionsgeschichte.* FRLANT 102. Göttingen: Vandenhoeck & Ruprecht, 1970.

Lohse, Eduard. *Märtyrer und Gottesknecht: Untersuchungen zur urchristlichen Verkündigung vom Sühntod Jesu Christi.* FRLANT 64. Göttingen: Vandenhoeck & Ruprecht, 1963.

Mack, Burton L. *A Myth of Innocence: Mark and Christian Origins.* Philadelphia: Fortress Press, 1988.

MacMullen, Ramsay. *Enemies of the Roman Order: Treason, Unrest, and Alienation in the Empire.* Cambridge: Harvard Univ. Press, 1966.

———. *Roman Social Relations: 50 B.C.–A.D. 384.* New Haven: Yale Univ. Press, 1974.

Marcus, Joel. "The Role of Scripture in the Gospel Passion Narratives." In *The Death of Jesus in Early Christianity,* edited by John Carroll and Joel Green, 205–33. Peabody, Mass.: Hendrickson, 1995.

———. *The Way of the Lord: Christological Exegesis of the Old Testament in the Gospel of Mark.* Louisville: Westminster John Knox, 1992.

Martin, Dale B. *The Corinthian Body.* New Haven: Yale Univ. Press, 1995.

Martin-Achard, Robert. "Resurrection: Old Testament." *ABD* 5.680–84.

Martyn, J. Louis. *The Gospel of John in Christian History: Essays for Interpreters.* New York: Paulist, 1978.

———. *History and Theology in the Fourth Gospel.* Rev. ed. Nashville: Abingdon, 1979.

Marxsen, Willi. "When Did Christian Faith Begin?" In *Jesus and the Church: The Beginnings of Christianity,* 76–95. Translated and edited by Philip E. Devenish. Philadelphia: Trinity, 1992.

Milgrom, Jacob. "Israel's Sanctuary: The Priestly 'Picture of Dorian Gray.'" *RB* 83 (1976) 390–99. Reprinted in idem, *Studies in Cultic Theology and Terminology,* 75–84. SJLA 36. Leiden: Brill, 1983.

Miller, Robert J. "Historical Method and the Deeds of Jesus: The Test Case of the Temple Destruction." *Forum* 8, nos. 1-2 (1992) 5–30.

Minear, Paul S. *John: The Martyr's Gospel.* New York: Pilgrim, 1984.

Munroe, Winsom. *Authority in Paul and Peter: The Identification of a Pastoral Stratum in the Pauline Corpus and 1 Peter.* SNTSMS 45. Cambridge: Cambridge Univ. Press, 1983.

Murphy, Frederick J. *Fallen Is Babylon: The Revelation to John.* New Testament in Context. Harrisburg: Trinity, 1998.

Musurillo, Herbert. *The Acts of the Christian Martyrs.* Oxford Early Christian Texts. Oxford: Oxford Univ. Press, 1972.

Nickelsburg, George W. E. "The Genre and Function of the Markan Passion Narrative." *HTR* 73 (1980) 153–84.

——— . *Resurrection, Immortality, and Eternal Life in Intertestamental Judaism.* HTS 26. Cambridge: Harvard Univ. Press, 1972.

O'Neill, J. C. *Paul's Letter to the Romans.* PNTC. Harmondsworth: Penguin, 1975.

Perkins, Pheme. *Resurrection: New Testament Witness and Contemporary Reflection.* Garden City, N.Y.: Doubleday, 1984.

Perrin, Norman. *The New Testament: An Introduction.* New York: Harcourt, Brace, Jovanovich, 1974.

Pesch, Rudolf. "Zur Entstehung des Glaubens an die Auferstehung Jesu." *ThQ* 153 (1973) 201–28.

Price, S. R. F. *Rituals and Power.* Cambridge: Cambridge Univ. Press, 1984.

Reynolds, Barrie. *Magic, Divination and Witchcraft Among the Barotse of Northern Rhodesia.* Robins Series 3. Berkeley: Univ. of California Press, 1963.

Robinson, James M. "Kerygma and History in the New Testament." In idem and Helmut Koester, *Trajectories Through Early Christianity,* 20–70. Philadelphia: Fortress Press, 1971.

Sanders, E. P. *Jesus and Judaism.* Philadelphia: Fortress Press, 1985.

Schillebeeckx, Edward. *Jesus: An Experiment in Christology.* Translated by Hubert Hoskins. New York: Seabury, 1979.

Seeley, David. "The Background of the Philippians Hymn (2:6-11)." *Journal of Higher Criticism* 1 (1994) 49–72.

———. *The Noble Death: Greco-Roman Martyrology and Paul's Concept of Salvation.* JSNTSup 28. Sheffield: JSOT Press, 1990.

Segal, Alan F. *Paul the Convert: The Apostolate and Apostasy of Saul the Pharisee.* New Haven: Yale Univ. Press, 1990.

Seland, Torrey. *Establishment Violence in Philo and Luke: A Study of Non-Conformity to the Torah and Jewish Vigilante Reactions.* Biblical Interpretation Series 15. Leiden: Brill, 1995.

Smith, Dennis E. *From Symposium to Eucharist: The Banquet in the Early Christian World.* Minneapolis: Fortress Press, 2003.

Smith, Jonathan Z. *Drudgery Divine: On the Comparison of Early Christianities and the Religions of Late Antiquity.* Chicago Studies in the History of Judaism. Chicago: Univ. of Chicago Press, 1990.

———. *Map Is Not Territory: Studies in the History of Religions.* Chicago: Univ. of Chicago Press, 1993.

Smith, William Robertson. *The Religion of the Semites.* Reprint. New York: Schocken, 1972.

Stegemann, Ekkehard W., and Wolfgang Stegemann. *The Jesus Movement: A Social History of Its First Century.* Translated by O. C. Dean Jr. Minneapolis: Fortress Press, 1999.

Stowers, Stanley K. "Greeks Who Sacrifice and Those Who Do Not." In *The Social World of the First Christians: Essays in Honor of Wayne A. Meeks,* edited by L. Michael White and O. Larry Yarbrough, 293–333. Minneapolis: Fortress Press, 1995.

Taussig, Hal, and Dennis E. Smith. *Many Tables: The Eucharist in the New Testament.* Philadelphia: Trinity, 1990.

Theissen, Gerd. "The Strong and the Weak in Corinth." In *The Social Setting of Pauline Christianity: Essays on Corinth,* 121–43. Translated by John H. Schütz. Philadelphia: Fortress Press, 1982.

Vernant, Jean-Pierre. "At Man's Table: Hesiod's Foundation Myth of Sacrifice." In *The Cuisine of Sacrifice among the Greeks,* edited by M. Detienne and J.-P. Vernant, 21–86. Translated by Paula Wissing. Chicago: Univ. of Chicago Press, 1989.

Veyne, Paul. "The Roman Empire (Where Public Life Was Private)." In *A History of Private Life.* Vol. 1: *From Pagan Rome to Byzantium,* edited by Paul Veyne, 95–115. Translated by Arthur Goldhammer. Cambridge: Harvard Univ. Press, 1987.

Wellhausen, Julius. *Das Evangelium Marci.* Berlin: Reimer, 1909.

Wengst, Klaus. *Pax Romana and the Peace of Jesus Christ.* Translated by John Bowden. Philadelphia: Fortress Press, 1987.

Wilckens, Ulrich. *Resurrection: Biblical Testimony to the Resurrection: An Historical Examination and Explanation*. Translated by A. M. Stewart. Atlanta: John Knox, 1978.

———. *Weisheit und Torheit: Eine exegetisch- religionsgeschichtliche Untersuchung zu 1. Kor. 1 und 2*. BHT 26. Tübingen: Mohr/Siebeck, 1959.

Williams, Rowan. *Eucharistic Sacrifice: The Roots of a Metaphor*. Grove Liturgical Study 31. Bramcote: Grove, 1982.

Williams, Sam K. *Jesus' Death as Saving Event: The Background and Origin of a Concept*. HDR 2. Missoula, Mont.: Scholars Press, 1975.

Wills, Lawrence M. *The Jew in the Court of the Foreign King: Ancient Jewish Court Legends*. HDR 26. Minneapolis: Fortress Press, 1990.

Wilson, Jack H. "The Corinthians Who Say There Is No Resurrection." *ZNW* 59 (1968) 90–107.

Winter, Paul. *The Trial of Jesus*. 2d ed. Revised and edited by T. A. Burkill and Geza Vermes. SJ 1. Berlin: de Gruyter, 1974.

Wright, N. T. *The Resurrection of the Son of God*. Minneapolis: Fortress Press, 2003.

Yerkes, Royden Keith. *Sacrifice in Greek and Roman Religions and Early Judaism*. New York: Scribner's, 1952.

Index
of Ancient Sources

ACQUISITION SUGGESTIONS
FOR THE CHURCH LIBRARY

Your Name _____   Phone _____